Hoof & Paw Academy Code of

Developed by Caroline Thomas

The following ethical values underpin the standards of my knowledge, skill, competence and conduct as a Holistic Practitioner and teacher as set out in this Code.

I promise to teach my classes with fairness, openness, honesty and integrity and I hope that you will enjoy taking part as much as I will enjoy teaching.

I Treat animals on a daily basis with kindness and compassion as a trained Practitioner in the following mediums: - flower essences, crystal therapy, aromatherapy, EFT, and Reiki

I continually strive to learn more about my fields in order to enhance and maintain my professional competence so as to be the best teacher in order to teach more students to provide a better world for all animals.

I will do whatever I can with kindness and compassion for both my animal patient and human parent.

I instinctively look to the animal for permission in the healing process and I treat both animal and parent with kindness and compassion by providing as much information to the parent regarding treatment how many sessions, and what to expect etc.

I am so grateful to the animals I treat and their parents as I learn so much from them.

I always consult with the animal's parent after the animal has consulted with me as to the course of treatment we are going to embark on. And **<u>ALWAYS ENSURE THAT THIS IS IN CONJUNCTION WITH THE SUPPORT OF THE ANIMAL'S VET</u>**

I work hand in hand with conventional veterinary medicine.

Every day I marvel at how holistic remedies can enhance the lives of our animals emotionally, mentally and physically.

Copyright Hoof and Paw 2019

For further support on your crystal journey☺ I can be contacted via

www.emotionalhealing4animals.co.uk

With Love,

Caroline xXx

16. WHAT MAKES HIM/HER HAPPY? (HOW WOULD YOU DESCRIBE HIS/HER MOOD IN GENERAL?)

TICK BELOW YOUR CHOICE OF CRYSTAL

AMBER	MOON STONE		
AMETHYST	ROSE QUARTZ		
AVENTURINE	SODALITE - BLUE		
BLACK TOURMALINE	TIGER EYE		
BLOOD STONE	SUGILITE		
CARNELIAN	TURQUOISE		
CITRINE	UNAKITE		
CLEAR QUARTZ	ZOISITE		
FLUORITE	CLEANSE		
HEMATITE	CHARGE		
JADE	ESSENCE		
LAPIS LAZULI	MOTHER TINCTURE		
MALACHITE	GEM WATER		

13. IS HE/SHE ABLE TO ACT OUT NORMAL BEHAVIOURS EG, LIVE WITH OTHER DOGS? IF YES WHAT IS HIS/HER RELATIONSHIP LIKE WITH HIS/HER OTHER COMPANION.

14. DOES HE/SHE SEEM PARTICULARLY UPSET BY CHANGES / TENSIONS / CONFLICTS? (IF SO, DESCRIBE HIS/HER BEHAVIOUR)

15. DOES HE/SHE HAVE ANY FEARS THAT YOU KNOW OF? EG HOW DOES HE/SHE RELATE TO OTHER ANIMALS / HUMANS/ VETS ETC

11. IS HE/SHE SLEEPING NORMALLY? (WHERE DOES HE/SHE SLEEP? IS IT SAFE AND SECURE?)

12. DOES HE/SHE ENJOY GROOMING/PLAYING ETC?

7. DOES HE/SHE GET SPECIAL ATTENTION OR DIFFERENT TREATMENT WHEN HE/SHE STARTS TO SHOW THESE BEHAVIOURS?

8. IS HE/SHE DRINKING / EATING NORMALLY? (WHERE IS HIS/HER FOOD BOWL KEPT)

9. IS HE/SHE POOING / WEEING NORMALLY?

10. DOES HE/SHE HAVE ACCESS TO OUTSIDE?

3. DESCRIBE THE PROBLEM:

4. WHEN DID THE PROBLEM START?

5. DO YOU KNOW ANYTHING ABOUT HIS/HER PAST? (EG. EARLY ABRUPT WEANING/ABUSE ETC) – LEAVING MUM EARLY

6. WHAT WAS HE/SHE LIKE BEFORE THE PROBLEM STARTED?

QUESTIONAAIRE TO FIND CORRECT CRYSTAL

1. DO YOU KNOW ANYTHING ABOUT CRYSTALS?
   Y / N

2. WHAT IS IT THAT YOU WOULD LIKE TO ACHIEVE FROM THIS CONSULTATION?

Copyright Hoof and Paw 2019

5 Piece Crystal grid

Place a crystal on each corner and in the middle. Place a photograph of your animal over the grid.

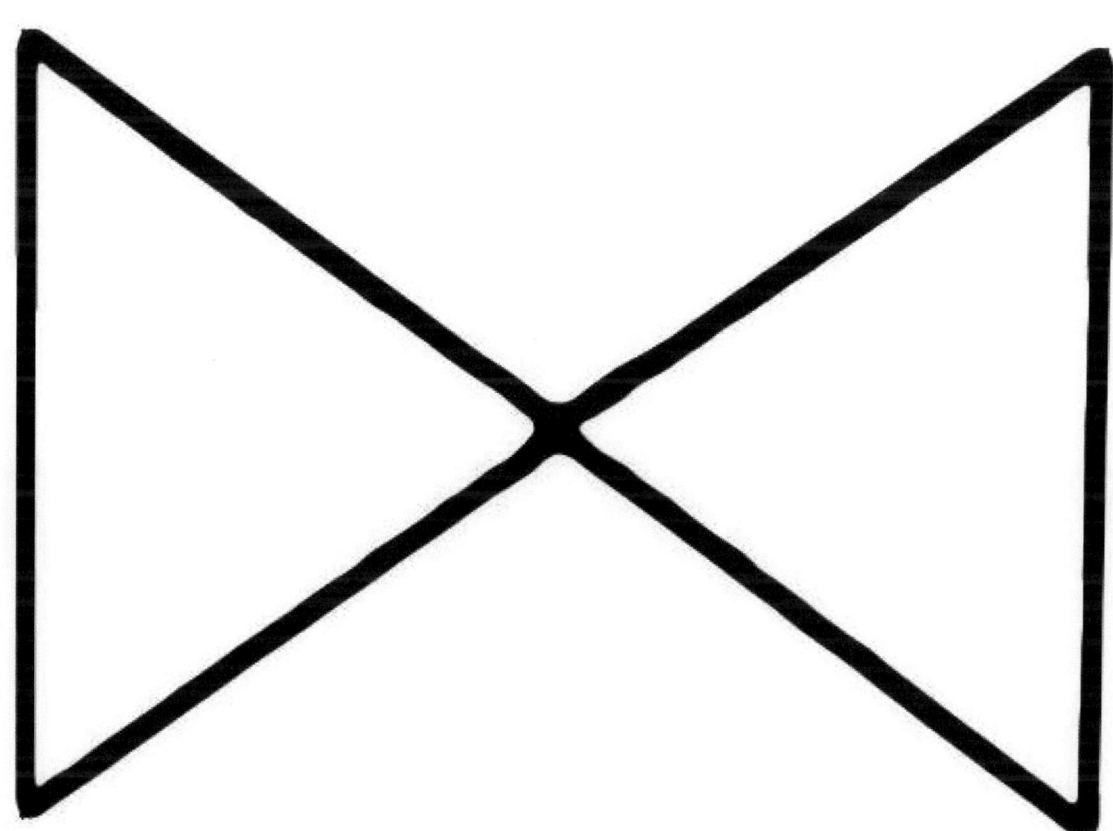

9 Piece crystal colour grid

Place a crystal on each circle. This grid is excellent for distant healing. Place Photo of animal above. Colour adds extra energy.

Copyright Hoof and Paw 2019

8 Spoke grid

This is an excellent healing grid, for distant healing. Place photo of the animal over the grid and leave for 7 days.

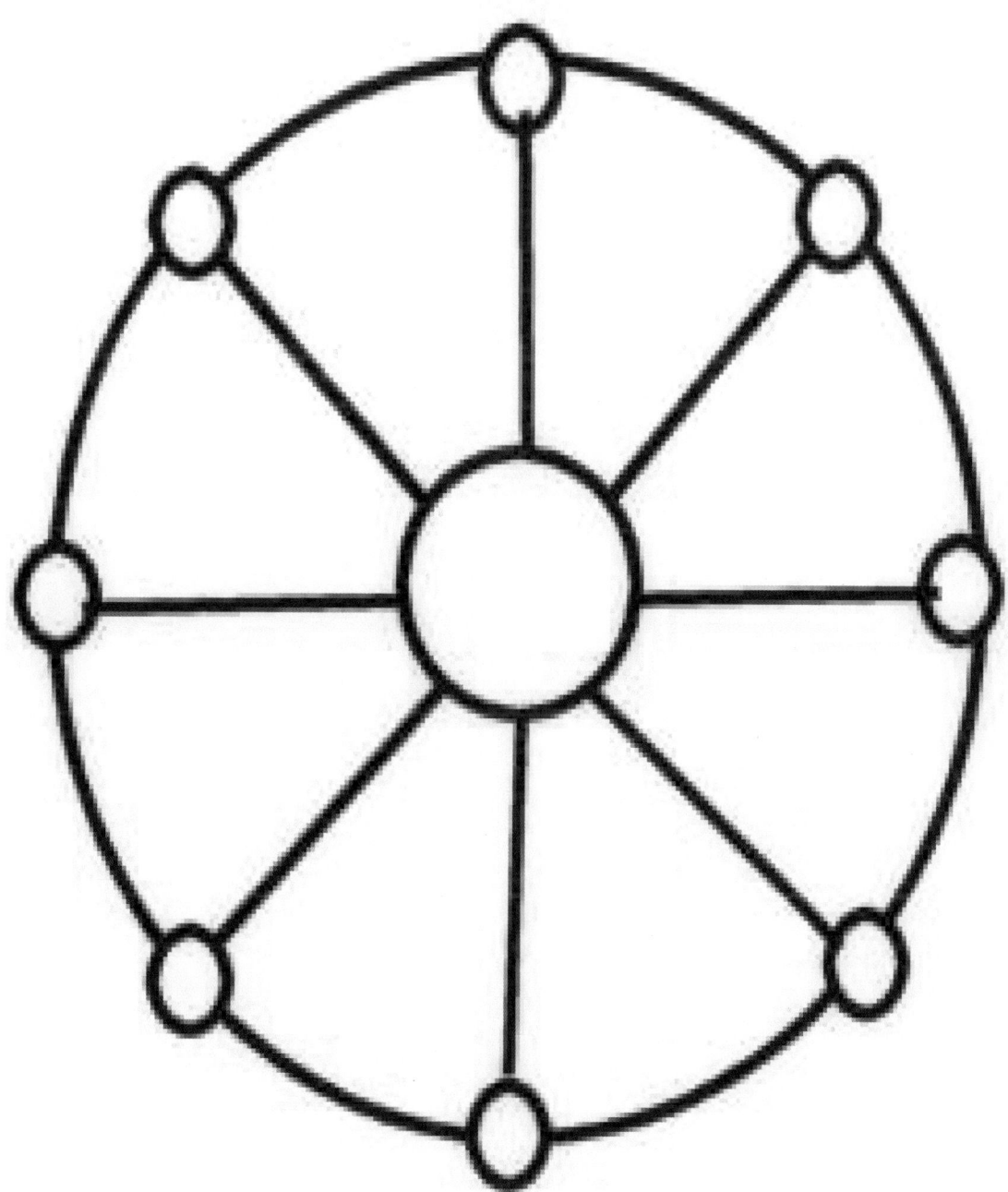

This is a very stable grid and enhances healing. Place photo of animal over the grid.

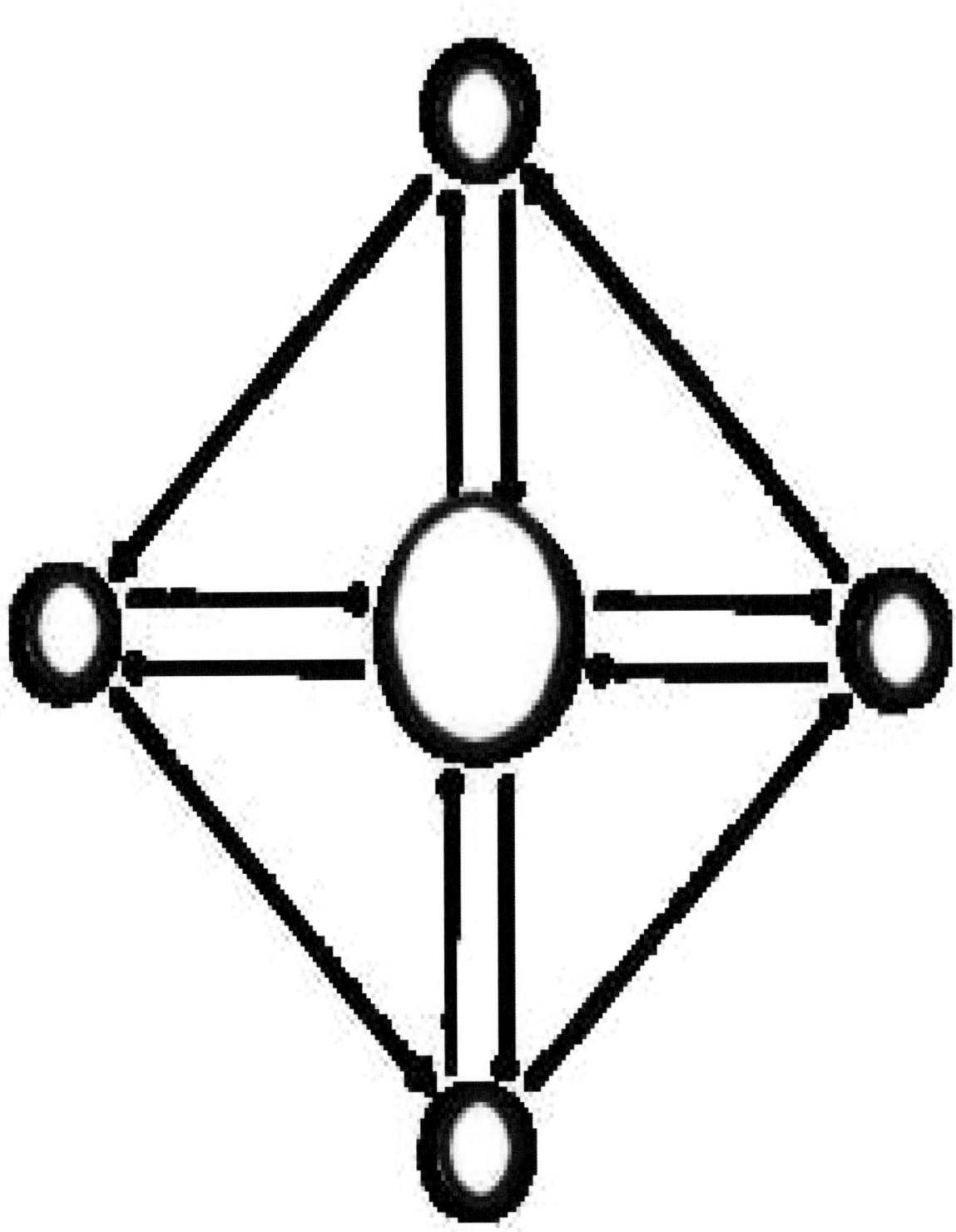

10-piece crystal grid

Place a piece of paper with the purpose of which the grid is being created under the central crystal. For a remote healing grid, you may place the name or photograph of your animal.

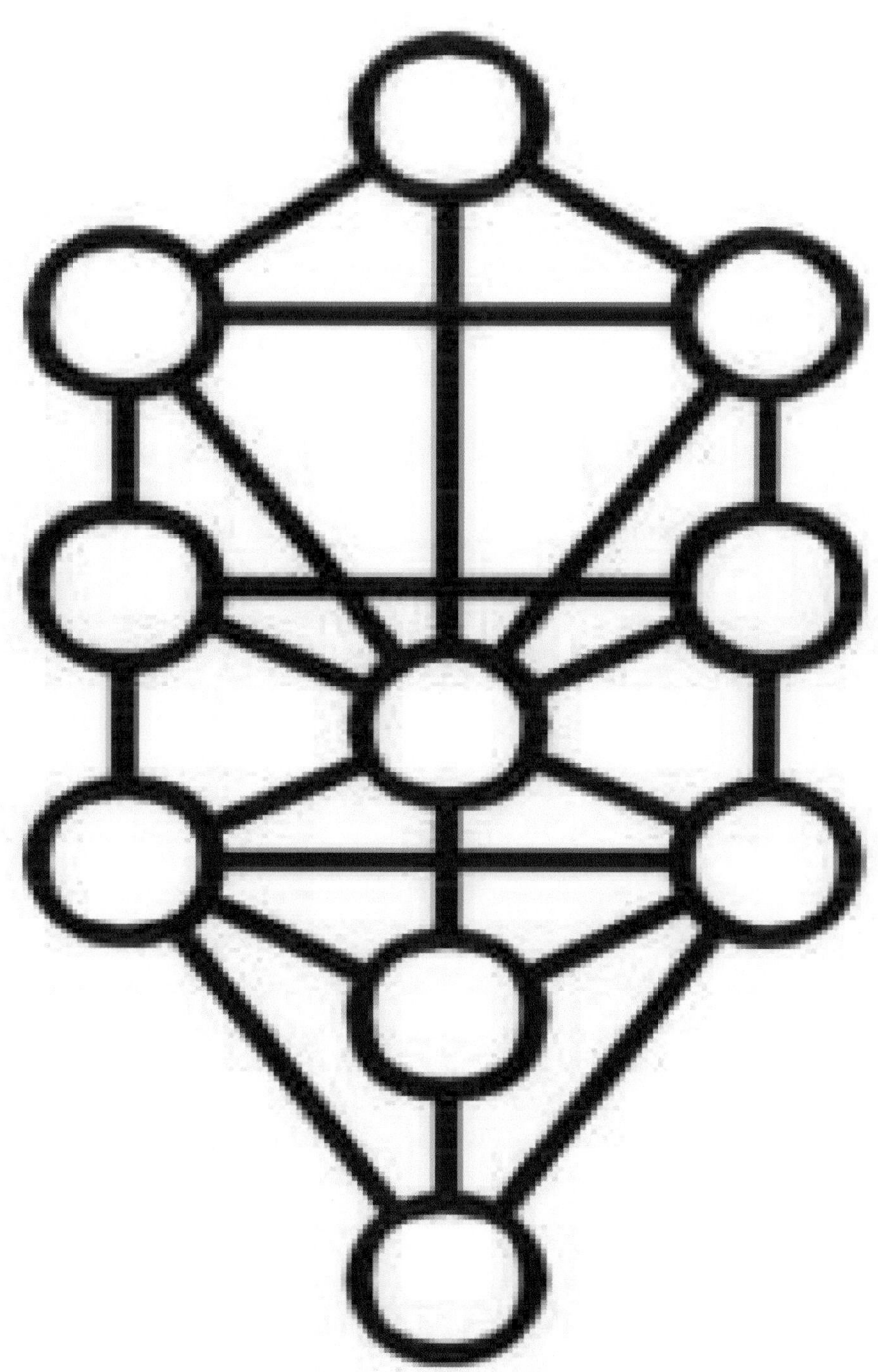

Copyright Hoof and Paw 2019

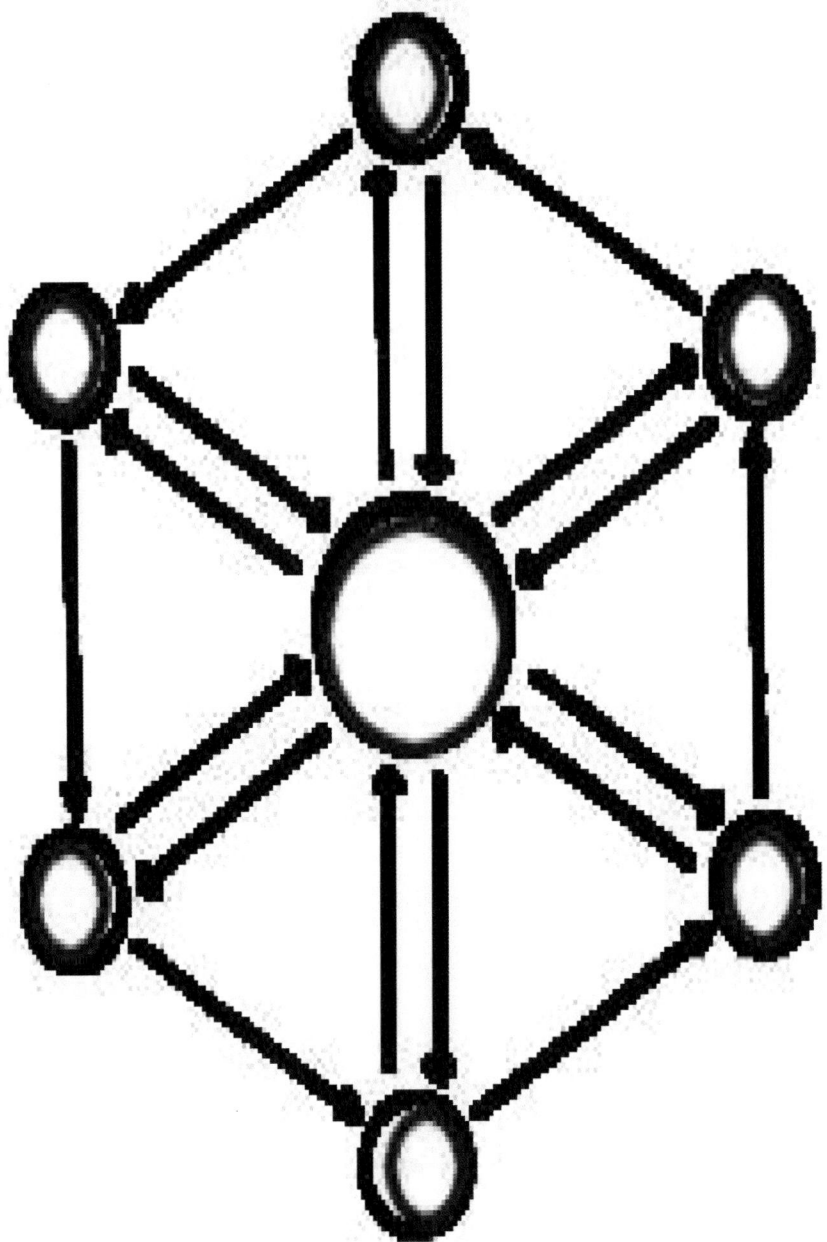

a

APPENDIX OF CRYSTAL GRIDS

Using the picture below as an example; try using the following listed grids. Start at the top and place the crystals on each recommend space in a clockwise direction. This grid is made of 8 crystals

the life of an old dog, who may be suffering from arthritis, for example, by adding amethyst to your crystal grid you introduce grounding vibrations which can reduce stress especially when an old dog is in weak health, and problems with separation anxiety. Selenite is often used to cleanse and remove negative energy from other crystals. It has healing properties that can help relieve tension and soreness in the body. This can be helpful for older dogs that suffer from joint pain. Black tourmaline is an excellent stone for dogs recovering from severe bouts of diseases. Amber has powerful  properties of protection and detoxification and is ideal for dog's that are suffering from various allergies and digestive problems. Amber is also an excellent stone to use for dogs suffering from anxiety and fear. Clear Quartz helps to relieve pain and reduce inflammation. Dogs suffering from problems with knee and hip joints can benefit from this stone. Lithium Quartz can help animals with low energy, lack of appetite, depression and if they have a history of being abused. Crystal healing is holistic and non-invasive. However, Dogs are a lot more sensitive to energies than us and crystal healing can sometimes be too fast for our dogs to integrate or be too intense and may cause pain and other discomfort. Easing off may help to alleviate the stress caused by a healing crisis. When healing is good, the animal will show signs of comfort and affection, such as eyelids drooping, drooling etc. Watch for tail swishing, foot stamping, ears back, teeth baring, hair raising, and attempts to flee etc. This is when you will have to slow down or stop the healing by removing your grid. Crystals, can have profound healing effects on our bodies and minds and can provide many positive benefits for our beloved dogs.

Crystal healing goes hand in hand with conventional veterinary medicine. This article is not meant as a substitute for seeking professional help if your dog is sick, injured, or you think may be unwell. Always seek help and advice from a qualified veterinary surgeon in the first instance.

Ref

https://en.wikipedia.org/wiki/Vitruvian_Man#cite_ref-2 "The Golden Ratio". *The MacTutor History of Mathematics archive. Retrieved 2007-09-18*"The Nobel Prize in Chemistry 2011". *Nobelprize.org. Retrieved 2011-12-29.*

Copyright Hoof and Paw 2019

Starting at the top right-hand corner (this is only my preference) place your first crystal working in a clockwise direction around the photograph, place the second crystal on the bottom right hand corner (again my preference) place the third crystal, bottom left hand corner, and fourth crystal top left-hand corner. Or as above, when using more crystals, I like to start at 12 (on a clock) and move in the same direction that a clock would. The last crystal is placed in the middle of the photograph. This crystal is the centre charger, you can use whatever you prefer i.e. clear quartz obelisk, or a geode.

However, you will want an excellent generating crystal in the middle to send out the energy that the other crystals have created. You can use selenite sticks or wands to charge the crystals in their grids connecting each individual grid to the centre charger, encouraging them to work in a unified field communicating with each other to amplify or transmute the energies of the grid in place. Imagine the crystals connecting firstly 1 to 4 forming a grid around the photograph then imagine them all connecting and communicating to the middle crystal with a whoosh of crystal energy. Always charge your grid during the full Moon (again my preference and it just means leaving them outside when there is a full moon). Quartz crystals are the most powerful amplifiers of energy. The quartz family includes, clear quartz, smoky quartz, rutilated quartz, tourmalinated quartz, citrine, amethyst, and rose quartz. Clear quartz is often chosen as its energy frequency is neutral and it can be programmed (which means you tell your crystal what you want it to do for you). Crystal grids can be reprogrammed if you change your intention. The most important thing is that your intention must have clarity. The greatest imperative thing regarding crystal energy healing is that the stones are thoroughly cleansed and charged. There are many methods, the most popular being water but remember that not all crystals like water and they can be damaged. You can also protect your crystal grid against unwanted energy fields that could throw it off by placing black tourmaline around the four corners of your grid. This is an optional choice and is not a necessity.

Before making a crystal grid it is important to check if your dog's chakra points are open or closed. You can use your pendulum to check. Blockages within your dog's chakras, meridians, and auras can be removed healing and harmonizing the body, by administering specific crystals. (This will be addressed in depth a future article)

Crystals resonate at a specific vibrational frequency, that attracts the energies of your animal's qualities and traits, for example if you want to treat an animal that has suffered abuse, Rose Quartz will energetically resonate with love and comfort, harmonizing their mind, body, and spirit, restoring calm and trust. My favourite stone is Aventurine, for enhancing love and positivity, when working with rescue dogs. I also consider Rhodochrosite, Rose Quartz and Sugilite. Crystals can enrich

Copyright Hoof and Paw 2019

programmed to relieve their emotional distress. This also equates to the need for crystal grids to be placed in animal sanctuaries, and Rescue Centres. You could also Place crystal grids in stables and when working with herds of animals outdoors, by placing a small crystal grid on top of a gate post.

In this article I want to take you through all the steps towards creating your own crystal healing grid for your dog. A crystal grid is an arrangement of crystals, tailored to your dog's needs. There is no specific patent to arrange a crystal grid, however I like to use sacred geometric patterns, as described above. This is designed to focus the universal life force for an intended purpose where the crystals have vibrational interactions among themselves but also with the aura, mind, body, and spirit of the dog that the grid is intended for. Grids can be permanent or portable. You can make a grid by placing crystals around your dog. However, this can be problematic, as you and your dog's energy must be very chilled, and there is a possibility of your dog ingesting the crystals.

A Simple Crystal Grid

The image on the right has 9 crystals in the crystal grid. The most basic crystal grid uses a minimum of 5 crystals placed around the corner of a photograph with one centre stone. Choose five crystals all the same type cleansed and charged. Try to keep the vibrational levels of the crystals similar as crystals are alive and vibrate at different levels, you do not want crystals cancelling each other out in the same grid, diffusing the energy field and allowing it to cave in on itself rather than being sent out to the 'universe'.

Find a quiet place, it can be in the same room as your dog, but it is important to spend around ten minutes looking at the photograph, imagining the image to be your actual dog. Have a loving and open heart as you hold the 5 crystals in your hand. Close your eyes and take a deep breath. Breathe deeply at your own pace, think of the healing intention for the grid you are about to make, take a few moments to think of this, infuse this intention into your crystals and send out loving vibes to your dog.

Copyright Hoof and Paw 2019

evil. Some think that sacred geometry is the way that the 'universe' speaks to those who would have the time to listen and take the time to understand.

The Flower of Life

The flower of life symbol has found its way into the human consciousness, it is no more than an elaborate extension of the Vesica Pisces, which is a symbol made from two circles of the same radius, intersecting in such a way that the centre of each circle lies on the circumference of the other. These overlapping circles eventually emerge as the beautifully abundant flower of life. If you draw your own flower of life, the energy of the grid will be very powerful indeed, as it will be filled with your own personal energy and love.

When making a crystal grid, I personally believe that a sacred geometric grid should be used as it allows crystals to communicate, in their ancient language which they can understand, this is ultimately connecting the crystals to the universal source energy.

"Crystalline forms are the key patterns for the way the energies are built in the universe: and the key is to unlocking energy in a constructive way" *Dr William A.Tiller, Professor Emeritus of Materials Science and Engineering at Stamford University*

Dogs sense what crystals can do for them and respond very well to the gentle non-invasive healing, shifting their energy, emotionally, mentally, spiritually and physically as they are closer to nature than us humans. I believe in self-medication in crystal therapy and this is done by your animal choosing which crystals are needed in their healing. You can also choose crystals for a particular condition or choose intuitively for your dog. Whatever method you use to choose your crystal you can also ask your pendulum for reassurance that the crystals chosen are the right choice at this moment in time. I feel that grids are so important for the emotional health of animals in sanctuaries, farms, and Rescue Centres. Animals who have endured physical and emotional cruelty and to address the welfare and emotional state of farm animals, due to ignorance and a lack of understanding. For example, although a calf would naturally suckle from her mother for nine months to a year, calves born on a dairy-farm are taken from their mothers within two days. This is done to reduce the risk of disease transmission to the calf. Professor John Webster describes the standard of the dairy industry practice, to separate the removal of the calf from the dam as the most distressing incident in the life of the dairy cow. This is where a crystal grid in the milking parlour and calves' barns should contain crystal grids

CRYSTAL GRIDS

As crystals are made up of a repeating pattern of atoms and molecules, which grow in an orderly and repetitive way. It makes sense that arranging the crystals in a grid formation will only enhance the molecular patterns that are already made. A crystal grid will amplify the energy of the crystals and the intention intended by the person making the grid. Intention is everything as to what you want the crystal grid to be used for. It could be set for healing, health, love and for numerous other intentions, the most important thing is that the crystal grid intention is set with clarity. If your intention is un-clear, then the results will be the same. Singularly crystals emit their own frequency but when placed in a grid a collective energy is achieved. This makes the energy of the crystals more powerful. Crystals from the same family can energetically communicate with each other much more easily than those from other crystal groups. This is because they are made up of the same molecular pattern so in essence they are speaking the exact same language.

Sacred geometric structures such as Stonehenge, show the significance of having stones arranged in a specific pattern. The makers of such structures must have placed great importance on these positions. This is an example of sacred geometry, which involves sacred universal patterns. These can be found everywhere in nature, and one of these is known as a **golden spiral** which is a logarithmic spiral whose growth factor is phi (In mathematics, two quantities are in the **golden ratio** if their ratio is the same as the ratio of their sum to the larger of the two quantities. That is, a golden spiral gets wider (or further from its origin) by a factor of phi for every quarter turn it makes.

$$\frac{a+b}{a} = \frac{a}{b} \equiv \varphi.$$

$$\varphi = \frac{1+\sqrt{5}}{2} = 1.61803\,39887$$

For example, the chambered nautilus grows at a constant rate and so its shell forms a logarithmic spiral to accommodate that growth without changing shape. Also, honeybees construct hexagonal cells to hold their honey. The **Vitruvian Man** is based on the correlations of ideal human proportions human proportions with geometry described by the ancient Roman architect Victruvius in Book III of his treatise De Architectura. Vitruvius described the human figure as being the principal source of proportion among the classical orders of architecture. Vitruvius determined that the ideal body should be eight heads high. The science and understanding of sacred geometry is growing more popular every day. The displays of mathematical and geometric constants are confirmation that certain proportions are woven into the very fabric of nature and can also be seen in ancient architecture too. Recognising the significance of sacred geometry offers us the means to understand how and why such matters were considered sacred. They and everything around us, are the product of the delicate balance between chaos and order, light and dark, good and

NERVOUSNESS

The biggest problem with animals that are nervous is that they have not been socialised to the modern world. There is a window of opportunity for all animals to be socialised to as many things as possible. This is usually between 8 – 16 weeks; they need to have as many positive experiences as possible. For example, with the vet, the hoover, the washing machine, being groomed, meet other dogs, horses and cats etc, Aventurine will help animals who are feeling insecure and nervous. Make into a gem essence (2 drops) four times a day for 48 hours. Use the direct method.

PAIN

Try to find out why your animal is in pain and if possible, the cause of the pain. Always seek the advice of your vet if unsure. Any type of pain can be relieved by using a clear quartz crystal. Take a crystal the length of your finger and point it towards the pain. Circle it in an anti-clockwise motion, as if unplugging the pain. Do this for around 10 minutes. Cleanse the crystal immediately after use. Malachite can be used for animals that are birthing. Make into a gem essence using in-direct method. Give (2 drops) four times a day when required. Sugilite can be used for severe nerve pain, make into a gem essence (2 drops) four times a day. Use the in-direct method.

PREGNANCY

In the throwaway society that we have, so many animals end up in pounds and are often put to sleep. It is our responsibility to neuter them, to prevent any unwanted pregnancies. Puppy farms are the curse of our society causing stress and unhappiness to both mum and pup. Horses and cats are also bred for profit without any care for the feelings of the mum or babe. In the instance of pregnancy Moonstone is the perfect stone for hormone changes. Make into a gem essence using the in-direct method. Give (2 drops) four times a day for five days. Unakite made into a gem essence will facilitate the health of the unborn animal. Give (2 drops) four times a day. Use the in-direct method.

SHOCK

An animal in shock can be unpredictable as they will instinctively go into their evolutionary coping mechanism. Don't over crowd your animal; offer them a calm space for them to recover. Black Obsidian can help your animal to return to a normal conscious level. It will help your animal to return to normal after a shock. Make into a gem essence and give 2 drops when required. Use the Use the in-direct method.

use crystals to check which chakras are out of balance. They maybe too open, causing your animal to be hyperactive. It is also excellent for extreme mood swings. Make into a gem essence (2 drops) four times a day, for 48 hours. Use direct method.

IMMUNE SYSTEM BOOST

Chrysocolla strengthens the immune system. It can help speed up the healing process during your animal's illness. Make up into a gem essence (2 drops) four times a day for five days. Use the in-direct method. Make sure that your animal is eating a good quality healthy diet and is not exposed to stress.

ITCHING

Amethyst relieves itching caused by infections of the skin. Make into a gem essence (2 drops) four times a day. Use amber when the itching is caused by insect bites/flea bites. Make into a gem essence (2 drops) four times a day and when required. Use the direct method for both. Amethyst is the best stone to choose as a flea deterrent. Wear as a pendent attached to your pet's collar.

JOINT PAIN

As our animals age it is often the case that they will suffer from some kind of joint pain. Green Tourmaline (direct method) is the most effective crystal for arthritis; it relieves inflammation and prevents the formation of degenerative damage. Use (2 drops) four times a day. Malachite made into a gem essence using the in-direct method (2 drops) four times a day, is excellent for rheumatism.

LAMINITIS

Blood stone made into a gem essence (10 drops) to be put into the horse's bucket every day for two weeks. Also give your horse another drinking bucket with normal drinking water. Use the in-direct method.

MINOR BLEEDING

As our animals go out and explore the world they can sometimes get into scraps with other animals, get caught in brambles and many more scenarios. Minor bleeding that is caused by cuts, scratches and grazes can be healed with a Carnelian crystal which has been thoroughly washed, can be placed directly onto the wound. Or made up into a gem essence, then dilute (20 drops) in 200mls of water can be used to wash the wound. Use the direct method. Seek the advice of your vet, if the wound is deeper or looks infected.

DEPRESSION

Sometimes, it is difficult to know if your animal is suffering from depression but if you have an animal that you feel is unhappy and your gut feeling is that they are depressed, Crystal therapy will help gently to bring your animal back to balance. If your animal is a Rescue Animal, then it is likely that they are depressed. Use Rose Quartz for animals that have closed hearts due to abuse or Citrine for animals that have given 'up' and have perhaps stopped eating. Make into Gem water (300mls) or gem essence and give (2 drops) four times a day for a week. Use the direct method for both crystals. Rose Quartz and Citrine can both be put into your animal's water bowl. Make sure they are big enough, so they are not swallowed.

FEAR

When working with animals, it is important to take the fear factor away from your animal if possible. Sugilite crystal is an excellent crystal for any type of fear. Make up into gem water (300ml) and allow your animal to drink from it. Use in-direct method.

GRIEF

Amethyst is an excellent crystal for grief, especially for animals that have lost an animal or human companion. Make into gem water (300mls) or gem essence (2 drops) four times a day for one week. Use direct method.

HEART PROBLEMS

Always seek the advice of your vet at the first instance. Aventurine encourages relaxation, regeneration and recuperation. It helps to keep the coronary arteries clear from deposits that supply the heart. Use Rose Quartz for irregular heartbeats. Make into a gem essence (2 drops) four times a day for two weeks. Use direct method for both.

HOMESICKNESS

Animals can suffer with homesickness, especially when you go away on holiday and they are boarding at a Kennels or Cattery. Use Amethyst as a gem essence (2 drops) four times a day. Leave with the kennel or cattery and ask them to administer it in your animal's water. Use direct method.

HYPERACTIVITY

Chrysoberyl helps with extreme hyperactivity in animals as it helps to balance both sides of the brain. It is also helpful to use the chakra picture of your animal and to

Copyright Hoof and Paw 2019

FIRST AID FOR ANIMALS THAT HAVE BEEN TREATED BY A VET

ALLERGIES

Amber is good for skin allergies, especially contact allergies, make into a gem water and leave in a separate bowl for them to drink from for two to three days or gem essence 2 drops four times a day for two or three days. Use the direct method. Remember that skin allergies can be a sign of stress, so reflect on the other areas of your animal's life, to make sure that all of their other needs are being met.

ASTHMA

Tigers eye and Turquoise relieve asthma attacks. Press the crystal hard against the chest area. Hold for 5 – 10 minutes. Use the in-direct method. Always seek the advice of your vet. Also, you can connect to your animal via your chakra picture and place the crystal on the heart chakra. Check with your pendulum as to how long you should leave it there.

BLOOD PRESSURE

Hematite stabilises blood pressure especially when low. Make into gem water (300ml) using the in-direct method or a gem essence (2 drops) four times a day for five days.

Amethyst lowers blood pressure when high. Take a piece of amethyst and starting at the head of your animal use a stroking action. Do not touch your animal then stroke from the head down along the neck, the back and down to the tail. Use a slow action and stroke about 20 – 40 times. Always start at the head with each stroke. Use the direct method.

BROKEN BONES

Make sure that the bones of your animal are fully set correctly before using a calcite crystal. Make up into gem water (250ml) or a gem essence using the in-direct method. Give (2 drops) four times a day for a week.

CONSTIPATION

Black Tourmaline eases constipation, especially if it is caused by animals that have travelled on long journeys. Make up into gem water (300ml) and let your animal sip the water. Use the direct method.

Copyright Hoof and Paw 2019

TWINKLY CRYSTAL EXERCISES

CHOOSING A CRYSTAL

Close your eyes and quietly meditate for a few moments. Then open your eyes quickly and pick the first crystal to which your eyes are naturally drawn to.

Run your hands lightly over the crystals. You will soon discover the crystal your hand will stick to, or the stone that feels hot or cool under your hand.

Use your pendulum and dowse for the crystal

FIRST AID WITH CRYSTALS

Sit next to the animal you wish to heal, a quiet undisturbed place is beneficial. Hold a Clear Quartz Crystal a few centimeters from the injured area.

Say the following;

'I am a clear and perfect channel for the highest realms of love and light, for the greater good of all concerned.'

Do this every five to ten minutes until until the pain goes away.

USING CRYSTALS TO BRING CALM

Sit next to the animal you wish to bring calm to, a quiet undisturbed place is beneficial.

Sit quietly and meditate with a Clear Quartz Crystal for about 10 minues.

Hold the crystal to the animals temples for about five minutes.

ELECTRO MAGNETIC POLLUTION AND CRYSTALS

Within the home crystals can be used to help reduce the effects of Electro Magnetic Pollution from equipment such as computers, telephone, televisions and any electrical equipment. As you can imagine, the animals in our lives are subjected to this pollution on a daily basis. Even horses, should we choose to carry our mobile phones with us.

Crystals adjust imbalances by absorbing the excess energy, thus helping your animals body's magnetic field to keep in balance.

Place a crystal near the television, telephone and any electrial devices. Remember to cleanse them frequently with one of the cleansing methods mentioned earlier.

YUMMY CRYSTAL RECIPIE COMBINATIONS

Rescue Dog Essence

- Rose Quartz
- Green Jade
- Aventurine
- Jadeite Jade
- Sugilite

Toilet Training Essence

- Carnelian
- Flourite
- Citrine
- Programme a Clear Quartz with specific instructions on toilet training

Mummy Dog is having a Puppy

- Malachite
- Unakite
- Moonstone
- Flourite

Scary Flea Essence

- Amber
- Amethyst
- Programme a Clear Quartz with specific instructions on telling the fleas 'This dog's not available for fleas'

Detox and Cleansing Dog Essence

- Black Tourmaline
- Malachite
- Turquoise
- Clear Quartz
- Smokey Quartz
- Lapis Lazuli

HOW TO GIVE A CRYSTAL MASSAGE TO YOUR DOG

What is a crystal massage you might well ask? It is massage that can be offered to your dog, without actually touching your dog. It is non-invasive and can bring relief from a painful injury. You will need a crystal 'wand', which you will be able to purchase from a good supplier. Always chose the wand you are drawn to. You will notice that wands come in lots of different shapes and sizes but will all work in the same way.

- To carry out a crystal massage you will need a cleansed wand

- Ground yourself & wait until your animal patient is calm

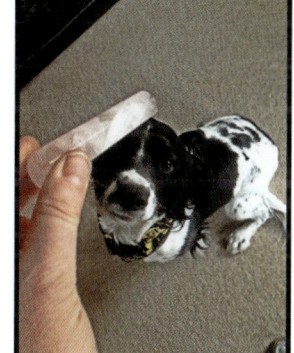

- Start with the round end pointing towards the animal

- Starting at the tail end move the wand in small anti-clockwise circles (un-plugging bad energy)

- Concentrate on the areas where it feels heavy

- When you reach the head turn the wand pointed end towards the animal
- Work your way back along the animal using small clockwise circles (Screwing positive energy back into the animal)

- When you have finished let the animal stay still or wander off

- Every contact the animal has with the crystal wand does it good

solution and I know that it is too much to bear, but knowing that you were with your beloved companion at the time of their peaceful and painless death, will help you through your grieving.

If you are preparing your dog for surgery, and indeed coming to terms with it yourself, the best tonic for your beloved dog is to spend every minute that you can indulging them with whatever they are able to do, things that they loved to do. If they do not come through surgery, knowing that we said goodbye and that our final moments were peaceful and filled with love is such a help when we are grieving. Their canine companions will be every bit as concerned as to what is happening in their lives, as they can sense what we are dealing with in the last days and months. Dogs are more in tune with their environments and surroundings, and I truly believe, fully understand when a canine companion is near to entering the rainbow bridge. Just like us, dogs have different personalities and display sadness and grief in a number of ways. for example, their depression can be displayed by loss of appetite, disrupted sleep or sleeping all day, withdrawn and feeling disoriented and clingy. This is so sad, and again we have to hold it together for our surviving dog who had bonded with their companion. In order to help our surviving dog with his grief it is good to keep a blanket or other reminder. Pay extra attention to them but do not go overboard as to create a separation anxiety problem.

Try to keep to a routine, and over time their grief will ease, and your dog's personality will return. However, if after a few weeks they have not resumed an energy for life, a visit to your vet would be advised. Give your dog some time to adjust to losing his companion before bringing another dog into the family as they are still missing their buddy and may resent the new family member.

Anticipatory grief occurs for us dog owner's when we begin grieving for our dog who is still living. We constantly ask the question? how will we cope without them? Experiencing, a deep sadness whilst holding it together for our terminally ill dog. This pain becomes acute when your beautiful beloved dog passes over and crosses the Rainbow Bridge. Give yourself permission to grieve. Your dog was a family member. Healthy coping mechanisms include crying, screaming, and taking all the time you need to come to terms with your loss. I advise my clients who are going through this tough road to take flower essences to get through each day from the start of this sad journey to the end and afterwards, until we can think about our beloved companion with a smile. Knowing that they will be in our heats for ever

we can, quality of life, relief from pain and discomfort and emotional support from us.

Our main hope for our beloved dog is an unassisted death at home, However, this is not always possible if their condition deteriorates. Holistic therapies work hand in hand with veterinary orthodox medication, for example Reiki, massage, acupuncture, proxy tapping, Flower essences and crystal healing. If they have a canine companion, they too should avail of holistic remedies to help them through this sad period in their life. As our dog progresses through their illness or dying in old age, positive emotions, enjoyable activities and more time with us is what they want and adds quality of life.

Chronic and Terminal illness can deteriorate quite quickly and an emergency house call service at a moment's notice or out of hours service at your veterinary surgery should be in place if euthanasia becomes imminent. Keeping a daily journal can help when discussing how they are with your vet. However, if they cannot breathe comfortably enough to sleep, stand or are no longer eating or drinking, incontinence, seizures, no interest in surroundings, how they tolerate medical intervention and vet visits and other symptoms that require constant monitoring and care, we must consider their quality of life, especially if they are in pain or distress. It may help to ask your vet what they would do in this situation? as we don't want to euthanise too soon if they still have quality of life and we don't want them to suffer by delaying it, by seeking advice from our veterinary surgeon hopefully it will help us to put your mind at rest as to whether or not it is the appropriate time to end their life by euthanasia.

Vocal or body language can be an indication of pain but not all dogs whimper in pain and it can be difficult to know. Lack of appetite and seeking isolation, lethargic, reluctant to walk and being grumpy are more outward indicators of pain. look for Subtle behavioural changes. Your dog may be losing sense of sight, hearing and smell and will seek comfort and security by being close to you.

Road accidents and surgery may take the decision of an unassisted death at home out of our hands due to complications during surgery. Your veterinary surgeon will always advise as to complications that may occur and discuss options that are available. It is of little consolation to us, but Euthanasia means good death. Your vet knows what a difficult decision this is and will discuss the process with you. It is your choice whether or not to be present when your vet administers the euthanasia

EUTHANASIA

When we take our puppy home, the joy, love and fun that we will have together are all that is on our minds. We go through all the stages through to adolescence and hopefully a full and healthy life to old age. Finally, we arrive at the time we dread, our elderly dog at the final stages of life. This is heart breaking and we have to be strong and hold it together for them as we will have to make so many decisions as to how our beloved pet is going to enter the Rainbow Bridge.

It is a shock to learn that your dog has a chronic or terminal illness and just months to live, but when you have gained composure, learn everything from your vet about your dog's condition. When we have a treatment plan in place for pain management and medication, our main goal in these final months and days is to give as much as

Apache tears:

This crystal has been used for the grieving process. It helps prevent further drain and damage of the aura. These beautiful black obsidian stones, when held to the light, reveal the tear of the Apache.

Selenite:

This crystal builds a connection spiritually that will remain. Selenite protects against negative energies and cleanses the area. This crystal may help you to connect to your dog. sleep with this crystal or meditate with it. Selenite connects us to the angelic realm.

Rose Quartz

Rose Quartz is excellent for relieving the feelings of grief and trauma. The energy of Rose Quartz is gentle, loving, and uplifting.

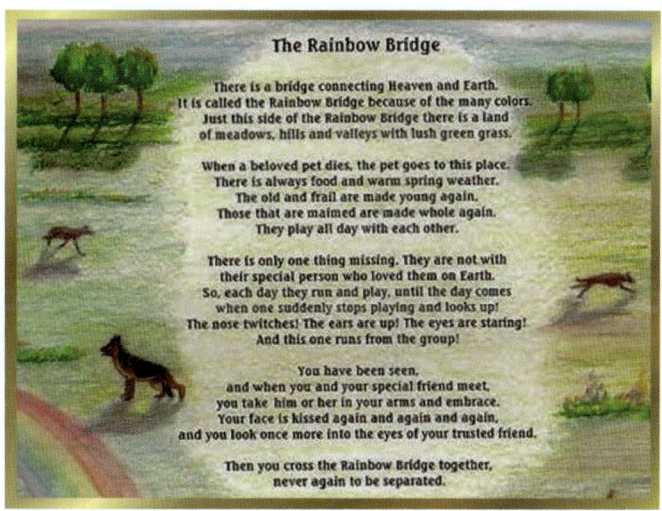

Amethyst:

In transition Amethyst is a very calming stone and will help your dog to relax and to deal with stress. Amethyst will help any companion dog and their owner to deal with grief and sorrow.

Ametrine:

In transition Ametrine induces a deep state of peace and well-being and helps to meet great demands with inner composure.

Blue Lace Agate:

In transition Blue Lace Agate calms anxiety, balancing your dog's energy and promotes sleep.

Carnelian:

In transition Carnelian releases sorrow and helps to lift depression. This is a sunshine stone and is excellent for animals that have a poor appetite and are feeling weak.

Clear Quartz:

This is a Master Healer. It is excellent to amplify energy, and when programming intentions it is able to hold onto your instruction for longer.

Selenite:

Selenite is helpful for transitioning souls, surrounding your dog with white light.

Jasper Red:

Jasper Red is a grounding crystal, which supports inner strength and tranquillity during times of stress.

Crystals to help their owner and companion dogs to deal with grief.

The death of a beloved pet is devastation triggering a feeling of emptiness, depression and grief. Humans and animals grieve in their own way. Crystals are a great help to us and companion pets to go through the transition of grief. Lepidolite carries strong lithium levels for balance, helping to diminish feelings of anger, sadness and anxiety. Keep it in your pocket, carry it and spend as much time with this crystal as you can. This crystal can also be placed by the companion dog's bed.

found on the nose, tail and ears. Whilst the bud and minor chakras are smaller energy centres than the major ones, they are every bit as important and assist in the function of the major chakras. The bud chakras are located in the feet and are often used to source areas of energy in the ground.

I find it best to let your dog choose their own transition crystals. This can be done by offering one crystal at a time by holding the crystal in a closed hand, allowing your dog to sniff the crystal. Hold the crystal tightly in your hand so that your dog cannot physically get hold of it in his mouth. If your dog is relaxed and sleepy, drooling, pawing your hand for the crystal, it is a sign that he/she is happy with that crystal. If he/she is not they will try to move away and will not be interested, so move on to the next crystal. This is a bonding experience between you and your dog, where you are both participating in the crystal healing session.

You can offer the chosen crystals by making a crystal grid, away from where your dog sleeps so that they can choose this space, if they want to sit in the middle of the grid. You can also put the crystals in a pouch on top of their bed or crate, on your dog's collar (if they chose) or in a crystal essence. Crystal essences can be offered in a separate bowl so that they can use their highly developed senses to take as much or as little of the essence that they need. Before you make your crystal water (which is basically leaving a chosen crystal in a bowl of water), cleanse and energise your crystal and set your intention. Always choose crystals that your dog is attracted to so that they attract the energies of your dog. Transition crystals energetically resonate with love and comfort, harmonizing their mind, body and spirit.

Suggested Crystals

Sugilite:

Sugilite is a love crystal representing spiritual love. It opens the chakras and brings them into alignment with the flow of love. It encourages positive thoughts, alleviating sorrow, grief and fear. Sugilite should be considered as the crystal to use during transition.

Rose Quartz:

In transition, Rose Quartz is for the heart, to help heal past abuse or cruelty. Rose Quartz helps animals to let go, and to facilitate harmony. Rose Quartz will energetically resonate with love and comfort, harmonizing their mind, body and spirit.

dog pain free and comfortable at home, through transition to end of life in their own time. Or to provide a painless, quick dignified death to a dog whose pain and suffering it is too much for them. Euthanasia (derived from the Greek terms meaning good death) will relieve their suffering for those that the pain and discomfort is too great, and medication cannot help. Crystals can play a big part in the final stage of your dog's life. Using crystal healing especially in the moments when the end is near, will offer a peaceful energy which will allow your dog to pass over to the rainbow bridge, letting go, so they have a comfortable death. In Death the aura and chakras disconnect and prepare for the soul to leave the body. Crystals offer support during this transition.

"The crystal is a neutral object whose inner structure exhibits a crystalline state of perfection and balance. When it is precisely cut to the proper geometric form and when the human (animal) mind enters into relationship with its structural perfection in the vibration of love, the crystal emits a vibration which extends and amplifies the power and grasp of the user's mind. Imaged thought intent is amplified." — Marcel Vogel

Crystals have been cherished by humans for millennia, from the Egyptians to the Aztecs. In 1880, French physicist Pierre Curie (Marie's husband) discovered that by putting pressure on various crystals – including quartz, topaz and tourmaline – he created electricity. This phenomenon, called the piezoelectric effect, is why crystals are used as essential elements in computers, TV screens, iPhones and satellites. LCD stands for liquid Crystal Display. It was the microchip, that contained Quartz Crystal, that truly revolutionized the world of technology and brought us modern computing equipment.

Crystal therapy is a non-invasive form of healing. All living beings are made up of energy and possess electromagnetic fields, known as the aura and chakras. Each crystal resonates at a specific vibrational frequency. Crystals vibrate at different levels; they emit a natural stable energy. Dogs are closer to nature than humans and are sensitive and receptive to the energy flow of crystals. Animals have an inbuilt knowledge of what they need which is also known as the hedonic response. They can sense what the crystal can do for them and respond quickly to the gentle healing. This means shifting their energy emotionally, mentally, spiritually and physically. My personal view is that dogs are already prepared to pass over to the rainbow bridge. It is often our grief that hinders their safe passage.

Crystals can be used very effectively to aid transition. Blockages within your animal's chakras, meridians and auras can be removed when using specific crystals. Dogs have eight major chakras, twenty-one minor chakras and six bud chakras. The twenty-one minor chakras in among other places are sensory centres and can be

CRYSTAL THERAPY, THE SCIENCE AND THE RAINBOW BRIDGE

Transition

Death is not the extinguishing of the light. It is the putting out of the lamp because the dawn has come.

Rabindranath Tagore

'Until one has loved an animal, a part of one's soul remains un-awakened.'

Anatole France

For me unconditional love is reciprocal between myself and my dogs – even if my dogs are sometimes a little aloof. The strong bond developed between my dogs and I is blessed with much love and happiness. Losing your beloved dog equally equates to the loss of a family member. Your dog has shared every single emotion within your family. They have not been judgemental or ever asked for anything in return. They are the emotional sponge, who have absorbed every emotion and have made it their life mission to listen to each and everyone's problems. The loss of your dog is a big loss and at the end of  their life we have a huge opportunity to be present, as they pass over to the rainbow bridge.

What is Palliative Care?

Palliative medicine is, by description, care that is delivered as a dog approaches his end of life. The most common circumstances that lead up to the decision to initiate palliative care include:

- The diagnosis or progression of a life-limiting illness
- The decision not to pursue curative therapy
- The progression of disease symptoms, so that they interfere with the activities of daily living

End of life palliative care begins the moment your dog is diagnosed with a terminal outcome. It is a stage of transition moving from treatment to palliative care. I have always believed, practiced, and advised my clients that veterinary care and holistic therapies work hand in hand. This is especially so, when you arrive at a decision between you and your vet and the final act of love as to whether you can keep your

The Conception Vessel and Governing Vessel Meridian

The Conception vessel and the Governing vessel are like midnight and midday, they are the polar axis of the body ... there is one source and two branches, one goes to the front and the other to the back of the body are two branches of the same source, and inseparable, front-and-back duality. Both can be connected when the tongue is connected to the highest point of the roof of the mouth. **Crystals:** Clear Quartz, Kunzite, lepedolite, Sugilite.

The Governing Vessel Meridian is yang in nature and starts from the uterus, runs down to the central region of the pelvis around the genitals and into the external orifice of the urethra in bitches and around the penis in dogs.

It passes by the anus, moves upward from inside the coccyx and sacrum and enters the brain.

The Governing Vessel also known as the "Sea of Yang Meridians" controls all the Yang channels. This is apparent from its pathway because it flows up the midline of the back, a Yang area, and in the centre of all Yang channels (except the stomach channel which flows in the front).

10. TRIPLE WARMER 	There is no physical organ for the Triple Burner system, AKA Triple Warmer, Triple Heater, Umbilicus. It relates to all of the organs and controls relationships between them largely through the endocrine glands and hormonal distribution systems. The Triple Warmer Meridian starts on the 4th toe of the front paw, it travels upwards along the front leg around the outside of the elbow, up to the shoulder, ending just above the outside of the eye. **Physical Imbalances**: Disorders of the side of the head, ears, eyes and throat, thyroid problems. **Emotional Imbalances** include anxiety, hypervigilance, fatigue. **Peak Hours:** 9 pm - 11 pm_Crystals: Mahogany Obsidian, Carnelian, Red Jasper, Mookaite Jasper, Clear Quartz, Fire Agate, Blood Stone, Sunstone, Hematite.
11. THE GALL BLADDER 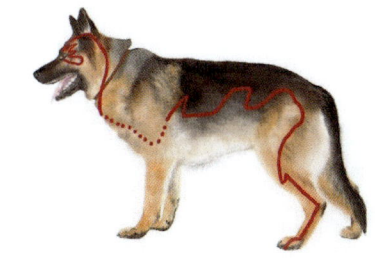	As the Gall Bladder Meridian starts near the eye, runs past the ear down the neck and then crisscrosses across the body to the hip and runs down the outside of the back leg, ending at the 4th toe. **Physical Imbalances** include insomnia, tendons, tears, nails, eye diseases, glaucoma, and night blindness, stiff neck, ringing in the ears, dizziness, weight issues, aggression. **Emotional Imbalances:** timidity, indecision, easily discouraged... and resentment. **Peak Hours:** 11pm - 1am Crystals: Calcite, Carnelian, Chalcedony, Citrine, Danburite, Jasper, Tiger Eye, Topaz.
12. LIVER 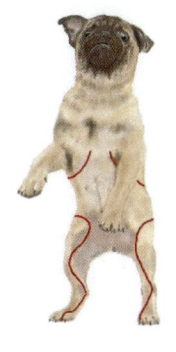	The Liver Meridian starts on the inside of the 2nd toe, up past the ankle where it then runs along the inside of the hind leg, through the groin area, along the abdomen and finishes just below the lung. **Physical Imbalances:** Liver function is reflected externally in the condition of finger- and toenails and by the eyes and vision. Blurry vision is often a result of liver malfunction rather than an eye problem. **Emotional Imbalances:** The liver governs growth and development, drive and desires, ambitions and creativity. **Peak Hours:** 1am-3am **Crystals:** Aquamarine, Beryl, Bloodstone, Carnelian, Charoite, Danbury.

Copyright Hoof and Paw 2019

7. BLADDER 	The Bladder Meridian starts at the base of the ear, a short distance from the eye and runs down over the top of the head and down the neck and the full length of the body, then down the back legs and ends at the 5th toe. The Bladder Meridian runs in parallel to itself on either side of the spine. **Physical Imbalances:** back problems, or urinary problems including excessive urination and incontinence, pain in the eyes, tearing and colds. **Emotional Imbalances** are Lack of energy, being inflexible and fearful - Resisting change and basic negative attitude are also expressions of Bladder Meridian imbalance. **Peak Hours:** 3 pm -5 pm Crystals: Blue Apatite, Blue Apatite, Garnet, Iolite, Kyanite, Lapis Lazuli, Sodalite, Sugilite
8. KIDNEY 	The Kidney Meridian starts under the main pad of the paw and then runs upwards along the inside of the hind leg towards the chest until it finishes just in front of the 4th rib. Physical **Physical Imbalances:** Chest pain, asthma, abdominal pain. **Emotional Imbalances:** Hysteria, paranoia, depression, fear, loneliness and insecurity. **Peak Hours:** 5-7 pm Crystals: Amber, Green Jade, Amazonite, Ruby in Zoisite, Unakite, Tiger Iron
9. PERICARDIUM 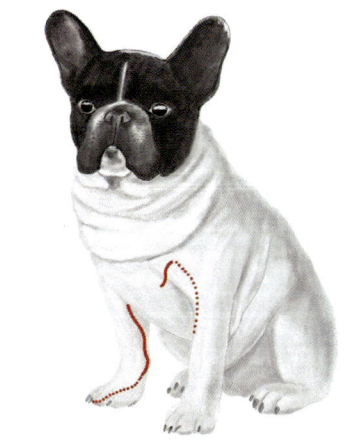	The Pericardium Meridian starts next to the upper chest nipple and runs alongside the inside of the front leg, ending at the 3rd toe. **Physical Imbalances:** Disorders of the heart, chest, stomach and mind **Emotional Imbalances:** Difficulty feeling and expressing emotions, depression, aversions, and phobias. **Peak Hours:** 7 pm - 9 pm Crystals: Fire Agate, Thulite, Green Tourmaline, Black Tourmaline, Clear Quartz, Clear Quartz, Green Aventurine.

Copyright Hoof and Paw 2019

4. SPLEEN 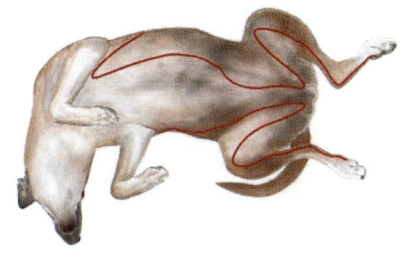	The Spleen Meridian begins in the 2nd toe, up through the ankle, past the Achilles tendon, along the inside of the leg, up through the groin area, along the abdomen, past the chest, ending in the 6th rib space. In the stomach, it sends a branch to its organs, the spleen and pancreas. **Imbalances** can manifest as food intolerance, weight problems, fungal problems, digestive problems. **Emotional Imbalances:** Worry, poor concentration, OCD behaviour, attachment (separation anxiety), stereotypical behaviour, jealousy, self-pity, stubbornness, low self-esteem. **Peak Hours:** 9-11 am **Crystals:** Amber, Blood Stone, Clear Quartz, Moss Agate, Peridot, Sun Stone.
5. HEART 	The Heart Meridian and the Spleen Meridian meet in the torso area and travels towards the underarm. It then travels down the front leg to the outside toe. As with everything of the heart, be prepared for a rocky road, a roller coaster of emotions. **Physical problems** include, chest, chest pains, shortness of breath. **Emotional Imbalances** are sadness, depression, fear, anxiety, hysteria, erratic behaviour, jealousy and sorrow. **Peak Hours:** 11 am - 1 pm **Crystals:** Clear Quartz, Rhodonite, Rhodocrosite, Rose Quartz.
6. THE SMALL INTESTINE 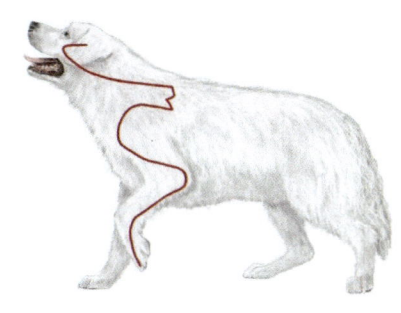	The small Intestine Meridian starts on the front leg at the 4th toe and runs upwards and then around the inside of the elbow, outside of the upper arm and shoulder at this position, it travels externally across the neck and cheek until it reaches the outer corner of the eye and then ends in the ear. **Physical problems** can include emaciation, profuse sweating, swellings of nodules, pain around the ear, and pain depressing the abdomen, digestive problems, knee problems. **Emotional Imbalances:** A feeling of mental deficiency due to inability to assimilate ideas, and insecurity. Forgetfulness, indecision. Restlessness and difficulty in expressing emotions. **Peak Hours:** 1-3 pm Crystals: Agate, Aventurine, Citrine, Fluorite, Jasper, Malachite, Peridot. Sapphire, Sodalite.

MERIDIAN	PROPERTIES & USES
1. LUNG	The Lung Meridian begins in the chest area and runs down the front legs to the dew claws. The lungs are responsible for every breath that your dog takes and establishing 'chi' for the whole body. **Imbalances** can manifest as chest and skin issues. **Emotional problems** may present as: disappointment, sadness, grief, despair, anxiety, shame and sorrow, sensitivity to surrounding space. **Peak Hours:** 3 am - 5 am **Crystals:** Amber, Amethyst, Apache Tear, Clear Quartz, Black Tourmaline Moss Agate.
2. LARGE INTESTINE	The large intestine Meridian begins at the first regular sized toe of your dog and follows a line along the front of the front legs, cross's over the shoulder and makes its way up to the side of the nostril. It is responsible for supporting the digestion and passage of food through the body. **Physical imbalances** may present as problems with digestion such as diarrhoea, colitis, colic. **Emotional problems** may present as sadness, grief, worry, holding on to past issues, guilt, regret. **Peak Hours:** 5am-7am **Crystals:** Blue lace agate, Clear Quartz. Fluorite, Jasper, Kunzite.
3. STOMACH	The Stomach Meridian starts at the side of the nose and crisscrosses below the middle of the eye, just above the cheek bone. It travels down the underbelly of the dog and follows the shape of the back legs until it reaches the tip of the 3rd toe on the hind leg. It is responsible for assimilation of 'chi' from food. **Imbalances** can manifest with problems whether it be physical or psychic food such as: stomach problems - abdominal pain, distension, oedema, vomiting, fungal problems. **Emotional Imbalances:** Anxiety, worry, poor confidence, feelings of suspicion or mistrust, emotional insecurity, 'pit of the stomach' feeling. **Peak Hours:** 7-9 am **Crystals:** Amber, Aventurine, Citrine, Blue Sodalite, Peridot, Red Jasper.

Copyright Hoof and Paw 2019

Metal Deficient

When Metal is deficient, the presenting qualities may include being unable to relate to others, loss of structure, feeling disconnected, melancholy, suffering with prolonged grief.

Metal Excess

When Metal is in excess, the presenting qualities may include rigid thinking, and a person may be unreceptive to new ideas, controlled and controlling, overly analytical, overly ambitious, unyielding. Rigid and snappish if needs for order and creativeness are not met.

THE MERIDIANS

If an element is out of balance, it will manifest both emotional and physical problems for your dog. When the flow of energy becomes blocked it stagnates. Meridians are the rivers that connect all the 'Elements together'. They are the invisible 'energy' cables that supply the organs with 'chi'. They stretch and wind and intertwine like rivers along the body of your dog. Like any river, if it is not cleared of debris it becomes dirty and clogged. It soon becomes a trickle until it is unable to flow anymore. If you look at the debris in emotional terms, this can be grief, anger, loss, abuse, setback or anxiety. Each emotion eventually and inevitably chokes the Meridian pathway until no 'chi' energy can pass. The wonderful thing is that Crystal Therapy can clear the Meridian path, so the flow of energy can be restored again. Crystal Therapy works by promoting a healthy Meridian System by encouraging the body to heal. Although it is important to look at the Meridian System. if you are working on ONE Meridian remember that it will have effect on the other Meridians. With Crystal Therapy, what you are looking for is 'balance' and this can be easily attained by using the correct crystal.

How to balance a Meridian using Crystals

On the following pages, there are pictures of dog, with their Meridians clearly marked.

- Use a Pendulum and point to each dog picture and ask, 'Is this Meridian out of balance in my dog?'
- When you find a Meridian, which is out of balance, you need to dowse for the correct crystal. 'Is this the correct crystal to use to clear this blocked Meridian?'
- Tune into your dog and on the Meridian picture run the crystal along the Meridian, imagining it un-blocking and chi easily flowing again.

Crystals: Amethyst, Carnelian, coral, Fluorite, Garnet, Pink Agate, Pink Tourmaline, Purple Sapphire, Purple Tourmaline. Purple Turquoise, Red Aventurine, Red Calcite, Red Jasper, Rhodochrosite, Rhodonite, Rose Quartz, Rub.

Fire Deficient

When Fire is deficient, the presenting qualities might include lack of joy, inability to speak, cold extremities, apathy, depression, exhaustion, inability to love, hatred, despondency, relying on others for a sense of identity.

Fire Excess

When Fire is in excess, the presenting qualities might include compulsiveness, desire for permanent joy, aggression, impatience, impulsiveness, going over the top, going too far, frenzy and over-agitation.

The Earth Dog

The Earth dog has round, well-muscled, broad physique with an overriding tendency to be fat. They move rhythmically yet heavily. They often have rather scurfy coats and feel fleshy to touch. They like routine, stability and don't appreciate change. **Suggested Crystals:** Amber, Brown Selenite Calcite, Citrine, Golden Yellow Topaz, Jasper Mahogany Obsidian, Sunstone, Tigers Eye, Yellow Jade, Yellow jasper, Yellow Sapphire Yellow Tourmaline.

Earth Deficient

When Earth is deficient, the presenting qualities might include loss of appetite, lack of metal clarity, over-thinking, worrying, needy, clingy, unsympathetic, easily led, lethargic, ungrounded, self-centered.

Earth Excess

When Earth is in excess, the presenting qualities might include being overprotective of others, smothering, overly sympathetic, overly responsible, obsessive, obstinate, stubborn, seeking sympathy, over-eating.

The Metal Dog

The Metal dog looks slightly angular with delicate features; they have small bones, compact muscles, with a coat that tends to be dry and brittle. They like structure and can often appear inflexible like metal. **Suggested Crystals:** Abalone, Hematite, Moonstone, Pearls, Pyrite, Pyrolusite, Selenite, Snow Quartz, White Apophyllite, White Chalcedony White Opal, Obsidian.

Copyright Hoof and Paw 2019

loud noise. **Suggested Crystals**: Amethyst, Aquamarine, Azurite, Celestite, Chrysocolla, Coral, Mother-of-pearl, Lapis lazuli, Lepidolite, Moonstone, Pearl, Blue and Pink Tourmaline, Sapphire, Selenite, Sodalite

Water Deficient

When the water element is deficient, the presenting qualities might include fearfulness, especially to loud noise, despondency, inability to stick to anything, poor memory, lack of will power, premature aging, loss of libido, feelings of anxiety.

Water Excess

When the water element is in excess, the presenting qualities might include recklessness, over-ambition, over-dominance, excessive sexual desire and jealousy.

The Wood Dog

The wood dog can sometimes look stiff or wooden even though they can move quickly; they have a muscular lean square physique, thick coarse coat and feel firm to touch. They like a challenge and hate to be blocked. **Suggested Crystals:** Agate, Apophyllite, Aventurine, chrysoberl, chrysoprase, Dark Green Turquoise, Emeralds, Green Agate, Green Calcite, Green Fluorite Green Jasper, Green Kunzite Green Peridot, Green Quartz, Green Sapphire, Green Tourmaline Jade, Malachite.

Wood Deficient

When wood is deficient, the presenting qualities may include lack of control, inability to plan, poor judgement, poor co-ordination, no purpose and depression.

Wood Excess

When wood is in excess, the presenting qualities may include over-controlling and they may overdo it. They feel stuck and inflexible and lash out in frustration.

The Fire Dog

The Fire dog has the 'electric' personality that turns heads. They stride out gracefully with elegance. Their willowy long neck, limbs and fine thin coat stand out. They feel soft and velvety to touch. They like excitement but once their fire has burnt out, they become despondent and lifeless. **Suggested**

THE CHINESE 5 ELEMENTS

I will try to keep this really simple, as the Chinese 5 'elements are a huge topic. As we move through life, situations and experiences we can become each element. The 5-element cycle is fluid and not static, to be in balance each element needs to support the other elements. All 5 elements are equally important and should ideally be in balance, even though they are constantly being challenged. All materials are made from a single or combination of the '5' elements since these are the fundamental components of life. If the 'water' element is blocked, then it would not be able to feed the 'wood' element, and this would have a knock-on effect of the 'wood' element not being able to feed the 'fire' element and so it goes on. Dogs can also be defined as having specific personality traits of each element that governs their appearance, disposition and behaviour.

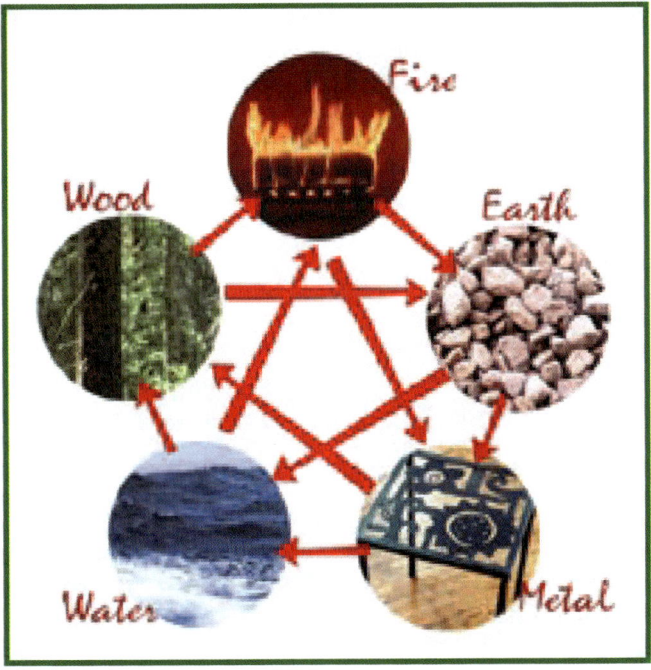

Below are examples of the overriding characteristics of each element. However, some dogs can be a combination of more than one element. Crystals can be used effectively to support the flow of 'chi' through the elements.

What is Chi?

Chi is the invisible aspect of the universe that is universal everywhere, it is the life-giving energy that unites body, mind and spirit. Everyone has chi, when you die, your chi is no longer there. It is timeless and part of everything around us. When it is strong your dog will have more vitality and better health.

The Water Dog

The water dog will have beautiful flowing movement, a glossy coat and tail, this is symbolic of water. They have eyes to die for, a strong dense lean physique, sculptured face, high forehead, long narrow head, deep set eyes, broader at hips and long sensitive legs. They are highly sensitive, especially to

Copyright Hoof and Paw 2019

another. The etheric double may however be separated from the physical body by actions such as accident, death and anesthetises. Amputees are evidence that the etheric double does exist as quite often they are still able to feel limbs that have been amputated. This is evidence that the etheric portion of the limb has not been removed.

Emotional Body

The emotional body is very thin and surrounds the body of your dog. As the name suggests it is to do with emotions, moods, self-acceptance and self-love. It is important to know that all past emotions, which have not been integrated are stored in this layer of their aura and will eventually manifest as disturbances and blockages, which can cause sicknesses. Energy is reflected in the emotional layer of your dog's aura and is determined by the chakras and meridians.

Mental Body

The mental body holds emotions, thoughts, and visual images. It is the subtle energy dimension of your dog's sense of reality. This is where experience, memories and thought patterns are formed.

Spiritual Body

The spiritual body is responsible for your dog's true direction in life. It holds the key to their purpose and the reason for their existence.

Copyright Hoof and Paw 2019

THE DOG'S AURA

Everything has an **aura**. People, plants, buildings, rocks, the earth and animals.

Dogs have four bodies on the subtle plane, just as humans do. These four subtle bodies, the Etheric Body, Emotional, Mental, and Spiritual Body can indicate what the animal is feeling or thinking, and whether it is healthy. The various colours in the layers indicate the animal's health on all levels. Pay attention to the Etheric Body of your animal. Any dark spots, spirals, or a broken aura suggests a health problem. This is where the vibrational essences can begin to heal. An animal's **aura** is simply an extension of its energetic essence. And just like with humans, an animal's aura can be weakened by poor diet, lack of exercise, lack of fresh air (indoor pets), lack of proper rest, and lack of proper veterinarian care. Additionally, an animal's **aura** can be compromised by an unhealthy environment, including negative thought patterns of its human owners (domesticated animals), as well as by human neglect and abuse.

Etheric Body Double

The etheric body double is responsible for vitality otherwise known as 'ki', which is distributed around the whole of your dog's body. It also acts as a bridge between the physical body and the aura. It is vital to remember that the etheric body is connected to your dog's physical body and they are not usually able to function without one

THE SCIENCE BEHIND THE AURA

It has long been known that everything has an aura, the ancient civilisations were very aware of this fact, yet it has taken the science to catch up to prove it. Science has proved that the aura of your animal is an electromagnetic field which surrounds them extending out from their body. The appearance of your dog's aura is connected to their health. A dog that is healthy will have an aura that extends a few feet away from their body but a dog that is poorly will have an aura that appears depleted. New ways of looking at auras with modern scientific equipment can show tares in the aura, which eventually go on to become an illness of a more serious nature. Western medicine is not interested in this new advancement and prefers to shy away from using the evidence from these new techniques. Spotting illnesses early on before they have presented in the body, is a huge advancement. Crystals can be used to help heal tares in the aura, as they support the aura to heal and repair. What you cannot see does not mean that it does not exist, and scientists have proved that the aura exists by using specialist cameras to capture its beauty.

Everything is energy as I described earlier in this book; what appears solid such as a chair, a table is made up of pure energy, which is vibrating a specific frequency. As the electron, protons and neutrons vibrate within the atom, they generate energy. This in turn generates an electrical field which forms a field around the object/body. This is known as the electromagnetic field which is commonly known as the aura of your dog. The aura acts like a shield and expands out intermingling with other auras and can be triggered by emotions such as love, repulsion, attraction and fear.

Have you ever felt this before? A bad feeling about someone that you have just met? You instantly know that there is something wrong with their intention, you have a 'gut feeling'. Your aura is connecting to their aura and it is picking up that things are not as they seem. Or Maybe you feel instantly relaxed with someone that you have just met? The brain uses a combination of emotion and logic so the aura acts as a detector. Newton said that the above examples were triggers which affected the aura at the vibratory level.

Dogs are definitely in tune with their aura as they can be aloof with strangers, or act like they've known them for years. We do not know whether dogs can see auras and if so, does this make them more aware of situations and new encounters? I believe that dogs are sentient beings who are in tune with their environment. They can make decisions based on how they feel and can make good judgements of their current situation.

hyperactivity, jumpiness as well as any related problems associated with the areas

Crown Chakra This chakra is usually represented as violet. The Crown Chakra: (violet spot on the diagram).
Influences: Cranium, right brain hemisphere, cerebral cortex, side of face, right eye.
Healing Crystal: Amethyst, Clear Quartz, Opal.
Healing Benefits: Use of the healing crystal on the Crown Chakra helps to alleviate confusion, senility, depression, malaise, convulsions, and any related problems associated with area mentioned under Influences.

appetite, increase energy, eliminate fatigue, and any related problems associated with areas mentioned under Influences.

Heart Chakra This chakra is usually represented as green or pink. This is to do with love and hate, compassion, resentment or loyalty. The Heart Chakra: (green spot on the diagram).
Influences: Heart, blood circulation, lower lungs, chest, thoracic vertebrae, immune system.
Healing Crystal: Emerald, Green Jade, Rose Quartz.
Healing Benefits: Use of the healing crystal on the Heart Chakra helps to alleviate heart and circulatory problems, immune system dysfunctions, emotional instability, anger. Energizes the blood and circulation. Instils harmony, balance, contentment, peace, happiness. Helps with other problems associated with areas mentioned under Influences.

Throat Chakra This chakra is usually represented as blue. It is linked to communication and expression. A dog barking too much could have an overactive throat chakra. The Throat Chakra: (blue on the diagram).
Influences: Thyroid, lungs, respiratory system, forelegs, paws, throat, mouth, vocal chords,
Healing Crystal: Blue Topaz, Turquoise, Aquamarine.
Healing Benefits: Use of the healing crystal on the Throat Chakra helps to alleviate depression, thyroid problems, barking problems, hair loss, abnormal weight gain or loss, problems with metabolism, and any related problems associated with the areas mentioned under Influences.

Brow Chakra This chakra is usually represented as purple. It is associated with fears. The Brow Chakra: (purple spot on the diagram).
Influences: Left brain hemisphere, side of head, forehead, ears, nose, left eye, base of skull, nervous system.
Healing Crystal: Blue Sapphire, Clear Quartz, Tourmaline.
Healing Benefits: Use of the healing crystal on the Eye Chakra helps to alleviate headaches, problems with the eyes, tension,

PROPERTIES OF CHAKRA'S

Base Chakra This chakra is usually represented as red and is situated on the base of the spine, where it meets the tail. The will to survive and to reproduce are rooted in this chakra. How secure your dog feels can also be seen in this chakra. (red spot on the diagram).
Influences: Adrenal glands, spine, bones (marrow), legs, back paws, colon, anus, tail, and kidneys.
Healing Crystal: Garnet, Ruby, and Smoky Quartz.
Healing Benefits: Use of the healing crystal on the Base Chakra helps to balance the physical animal body and clear out fears, insecurity, and anger. Helps to relieve spinal tension, constipation, anemia's, urinary incontinence, and any related problems associated with the areas mentioned under Influences.

Sacral Chakra This chakra is usually represented as orange. It corresponds to the reproductive system, sexual drive and function. The Sacral Chakra: (orange spot on the diagram).
Influences: Genitals, pelvis, reproductive organs, large and small intestines, stomach, sacrum, and lumbar vertebrae.
Healing Crystal: Moonstone, Topaz, and Opal.
Healing Benefits: Use of the healing crystal on the Sacral Chakra helps to release tension, relieve sexual difficulties, increase male potency, heal problems with the uterus or bladder, impotence, and any related problems associated with the areas mentioned under Influences.

Solar Plexus This chakra is usually represented as yellow. It also represents how much control your dog feels that they have over their life. The Solar Plexus Chakra: (yellow spot on the diagram).
Influences: Stomach, gallbladder, pancreas, liver, diaphragm, kidneys, nervous system, and lumbar vertebrae.
Healing Crystal: Tiger Eye, Amber, Citrine
Healing Benefits: Use of the healing crystal on the Solar Plexus Chakra helps to clear digestive disorders, increase

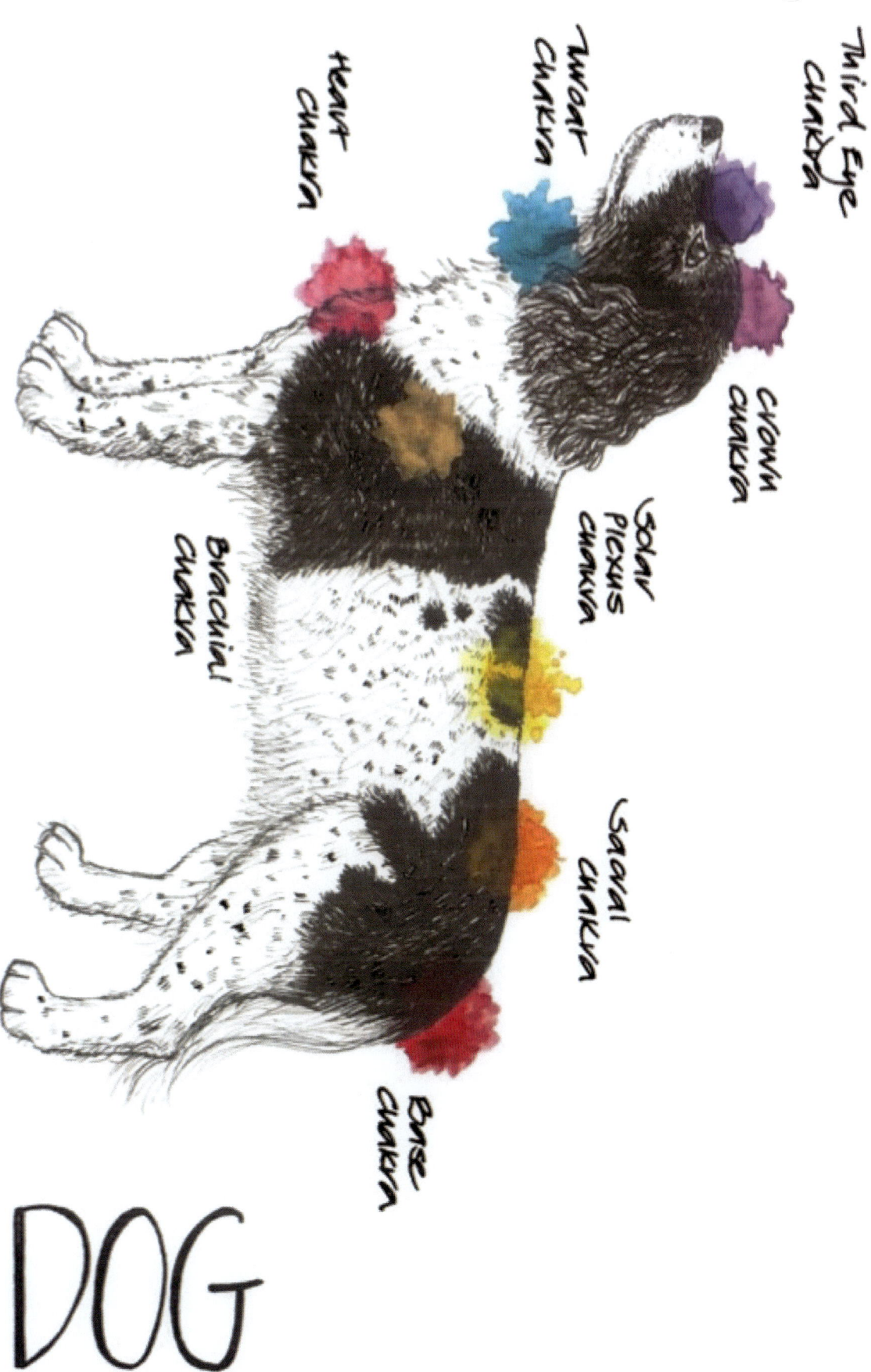

THINK OF YOUR DOG WELL

The Power of Positive Thinking. On the surface, your dog may appear to have all of their needs met, but fundamentally there still may be an underlying problem with their health. They have taken their crystal essences correctly, and emotionally they are improving, yet there is still something wrong. I get lots of emails from people saying, "My vet cannot find anything wrong, yet my dog has weight issues, even though he is on a strict diet!" or "My dog keeps chewing my kitchen chairs while I am at work, how do I stop him?"

Sometimes without realising it, our dogs can manifest what we are actually thinking. If you are worried about your dog putting on weight, they won't get the message "stop putting on weight", the message will be "weight". Just like if a dog is digging in the garden, they won't get the message "stop digging", they will just get the message "digging" … and they will think oh yes, my owner wants me to "dig". If you do have a problem with your dog that has no cause and the vet is unable to find a problem – Stop! And take stock and mentally take a note of the signals you have been giving your dog. What is your thought process when you talk about your dog? What benefits could there be for you/

When our dogs are chronically sick, the kindest thing we can do is to be optimistic. We need to see past their ailing body and to visualise them as fit and healthy. We need to let go of feelings of sorrow and pity and to understand that dogs think differently to us. This is especially very important when we think of rescue animals, they need us to see them at the best they can possibly be. Visualise them with a happy new owner who has given them their forever home.

Use Positive Thinking and visualise your animal to wellness

1. Find somewhere comfortable and quiet to connect to your animal
2. Close your eyes and visualise your animal looking happy and healthy
3. Imagine them being playful and blissfully injury free
4. Feel with your whole heart that they make a 100% recovery
5. Thank them and believe (belief is the magical key)

The words that we say and the energy that we say them with are picked up by our dogs, just like a sponge absorbing water. The way we see and perceive our dog is again picked up by our dogs and taken on board to their very psyche. Little changes to your thought process can have a huge impact on the well-being of your dog. Give it a go and be prepared to be amazed.

HOW TO BALANCE YOUR DOG'S CHAKRA'S

This is where you have to take a leap of faith and trust in something you cannot see or feel. The best way to describe the chakras of your dog, is to imagine them as 'energy' centres, taking in good energy from your dog's surroundings. They open and close up to their environment, depending on how your dog is feeling. Your dog has 7 chakra's running along the spine of their body. **Starting** at the tail and finishing at the top of their head. If one of their chakras is too open and letting in too much energy, then they may be overactive. Also, if a chakra is blocked or too closed and not letting in enough energy, then your dog may feel lethargic. In reality we cannot see whether a chakra is open or closed but luckily, we can ask our 'pendulum' to find out for us.

Using the diagram on page 45

- Spend around 10 minutes connecting to your dog, keep looking at the diagram and keep connecting until your dog and image become **one.** A picture of your dog can be very helpful, if your dog is not around

- With your pendulum in one hand, start at the base chakra by placing a finger from your other hand actually on the base chakra of the diagram. Always keep your dog at the forefront of your mind. In essence, it is not the diagram you are connecting to, but it **is** actually your dog

- Ask the question; 'Is this chakra in balance?' Wait for your pendulum to move in a 'YES' or 'NO' answer. It is important not to force your pendulum.

- If the answer is 'NO' then place a crystal of the corresponding colour on the chakra spot

- Work your way along the spine until you get to the crown chakra, placing crystals on any 'NO' answers

- Leave crystals in place and only take the crystal away when your pendulum gives you a 'YES' answer

HOW TO USE A PENDULUM

Using a pendulum, will allow you to not only choose the correct crystal for your dog but it will allow you find out what is going on with your dog at a deeper level. Learning how to use a pendulum correctly will help both you and your dog to make the right choice. For example, it will help you to choose the correct crystal, dog food, the correct vet and everything else in your dog's life with a 'YES' or 'NO' answer. The correct term for using a pendulum is called 'dowsing' I will be honest and say that no one really knows how a pendulum works and if they do, it is usually VERY complicated to understand.

- Purchase a pendulum that you feel drawn to
- Cleanse and Charge it as previously explained, beware however of the chain as saltwater will make it go rusty
- Spend a few moments in a quiet relaxing state
- Hold the top of the chain in your dominant hand and ask the pendulum, show me 'YES' wait for a response, as your pendulum will swing in a certain way unique to you. This will always be your 'YES' answer from now on
- Again, hold the top of the chain and ask the pendulum to show me 'NO' wait for a response. Again, your pendulum will swing in another unique way, which will always be your 'NO' answer from now on

Examples of uses for a pendulum
Ask only questions with a 'YES' or 'NO' questions?
- When choosing a crystal ask; 'is the right crystal for my dog?' Will this crystal treat my dog's allergy?
- Does my crystal need cleansing?
- Does my crystal need charging?
- Is my dog's base chakra out of balance?

Making a Crystal Grid not around a Dog bed

I have actually found that making a crystal around an animal is not always the best way to approach crystal healing. I have found that if you make a grid that is actually not around the dog and where they sleep that they will actually choose their own healing, when they need it and for how long they need it.

- Chose 4 crystals of the same type, depending on the healing situation you would like to address
- The crystals must be cleansed and charged
- Hold the crystals in your hand with a loving feeling or intention of what you want to heal
- Find a place that is not near your dog's bed (see image below, where the blue arrow is;) place the first crystal, then place each in a clockwise direction
- Visualize all of the crystals connecting together to form a grid, with a beautiful loving energy.

Copyright Hoof and Paw 2019

CRYSTAL GRIDS

When it comes to crystal grids, it is here that I have found the best way to use them with animals, is actually to have a photograph of the dog you want to work with. You can of course place crystals around your dog and I have used this method often, but you always have to choose the right time, which is basically when your  dog is asleep or very settled. The energy of both you and your dog has to be very chilled; I have found that even getting up, whilst they are asleep to place your crystals around them usually disturbs them. This is because dogs are always primed ready for action, if danger should occur. You have to remember that your dog is naturally on guard for any sounds or any danger that may occur. They are the protector of your home.

Making a Crystal Grid around a Photograph of your dog

- Choose a nice photograph of your dog; preferably on their own
- Choose 5 crystals all the same type. They must have been cleansed and charged as explained previously. Choose them to depend on what issue you would like to heal.
- Find a quiet place, it can even be in the room that your dog is
- This is the **important** bit; spend around 10 minutes looking at the photograph, imagining the image to be your actual dog
- Have a loving and open heart as you hold the 5 crystals in your hand
- Starting on the top right-hand corner (this is only my preferences) place your first crystal there
- Working in a clockwise direction place the second crystal on the bottom right hand corner (again my preference)
- Third crystal, bottom left hand corner, forth crystal top left-hand corner
- Now the last crystal is placed in the middle of the photograph
- Imagine the crystals connecting, firstly 1 to 4 forming a grid around the photograph then imagine them **ALL** connecting to the middle crystal…. With a whoosh of crystal energy.
- How long should you leave the crystal grid in place? This can be dependent on your gut feeling or you can ask your pendulum too.

Copyright Hoof and Paw 2019

Do Crystal Essences Change Your Dog Permanently?

They will enhance the opportunity for change in your animal, so it is important to look at the whole picture and enhance the healing process of your animal. If you do not change the environment that is causing stress or anxiety to your animal, your animal will not have the opportunity to change and will therefore go back to their negative behaviour.

For How Long Can I give the Crystal Essence to My Dog?

Response to Crystal Essences varies from the first initial seconds or minutes to many weeks, depending on your animal's sensitivity. I would recommend not giving the Essence any longer than 30 – 60 days. You should have noticed some change in your animal's behaviour.

Are Crystal Essences Safe to Use with Veterinary Medicine?

Crystal Essences **cannot** interact with Western Medicine because they contain the 'energy' of the Crystal. They can be added to creams, mixtures, compresses and any washes. Crystal Essences can be used alongside or combined with any other healing therapy with **no** adverse problems.

Is it harmful for my other pets to drink water with essences?

This is a question that I am asked often, so I will answer it as best I can. As Crystal Essences are the 'energy' of the Crystal they contain **no** component of the Crystal therefore they have no harmful side effects. However, I would give them individually to your animal and not put the Crystal Essence in the communal water bowl.

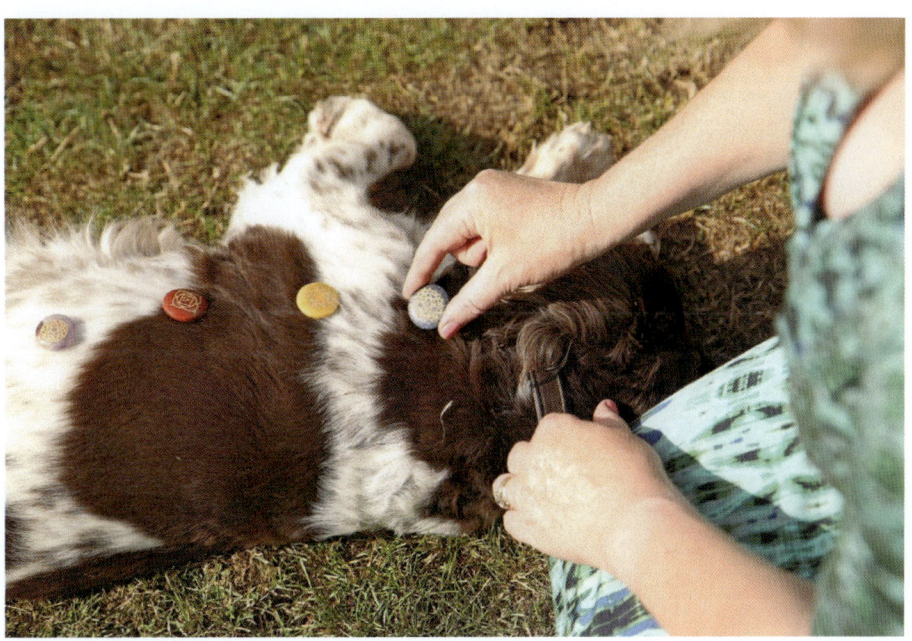

Copyright Hoof and Paw 2019

Crystal Essences in Depth

'Crystal Essences affect the mind, body, spirit and physical body of your animal'

How Do Crystal Essences work?

One drop or one gallon will have the same effect; it is the frequency with which the Essences is given and not the quantity. Crystal Essences are known as 'vibrational medicines' which means that they will raise the vibration of your animal. Almost everything around us has a living pulse inside of it, which vibrates at its own unique frequency. Vibrational Medicines work on the principle that like attracts like. When the G string of a guitar is plucked, all the other octave strings of G begin to vibrate. They are in resonance with one another. The different parts of our physical, emotional, mental and spiritual being resonate to various frequencies of vibration. The Harmonic Scale of Emotion, as described by Robert Tennyson Stevens, indicates which emotions are high frequencies and which ones are not. The highest frequency emotion is enthusiasm; love and joy also fall into this category. This is followed by pain (emotional or physical) which is followed by anger. The next lower frequency emotion is fear, which is followed by grief. Below grief is apathy. Finally, the lowest frequency emotion is unconsciousness (meaning it is so awful we have completely blocked out those situations from our lives).

Disharmony shows up in the energy field before it becomes a problem in the body. Animals suffer from the same emotional problems as people. They grieve, they get depressed and many more emotions. These cause imbalances, which if detected using science can be seen in the animal's aura. If this is not addressed and the animal suffers grief from the loss of a loved one theoretically, he/she may go on to develop for example a heart problem, tumour etc. All emotional problems vibrate at a lower frequency and each emotion vibrates at its own unique frequency. By using a vibrational medicine to address this emotional problem, it raises the vibration to treat the grief so the disease can be avoided altogether. If the grief is never addressed and the tumour removed, it will possibly grow back again.

By raising your 'Animals' vibration you are therefore able to remove emotions such a grief, fear and apathy with emotions of love, joy and enthusiasm.

GEM ELIXIR PLAN

WHAT ITEMS DO I NEED?

- ....
- ....
- ....
- ....
- ....

DATE STARTED
....

STONES I MAY NEED

- ....
- ....
- ....
- ....

THOUGHTS OF INSPIRATION

- ....
- ....
- ....

OTHER THINGS I MAY NEED

- ....
- ....
- ....
- ....
- ....
- ....

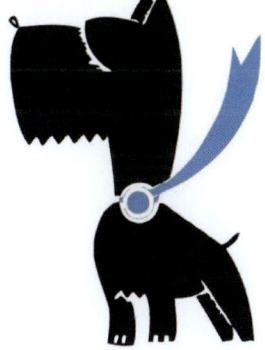

Copyright Hoof and Paw 2019

HOW TO MAKE A CRYSTAL ESSENCE (MOTHER TINCTURE)

If you feel that you would like to keep your crystal water and make it up into the mother tincture, you will need a carrier of some kind to preserve your water.

- Sterilize a 30ml dropper bottle.
- Pour the crystal water into a 30ml dropper bottle up to around halfway (15ml). The excess can be stored in the fridge and used over the next 48 hours.
- Then add the same amount again of brandy or cider vinegar to preserve your mother tincture. Storing this in a cool place, will keep the mother tincture indefinitely.
- Secure the cap and label with the date, name of crystal and any other instructions you would like to use.
- From this mother tincture, you will be able to make up a 'stock bottle' for your dog. Add 2 drops of the mother tincture to a 30ml dropper bottle filled with boiled and cooled water to the 15ml mark, then top this up with brandy or cider vinegar, you now you have your stock bottle.

- This is the fun part as you can add drops from your 'stock bottles' to make up a combination of crystal essences. Add two drops from each stock bottle (use a maximum of 7 different types of crystal stock bottles. The 2 drops are added to a 30ml dropper bottle that has been filled with boiled cooled water. This is now known as the 'treatment bottle') – less is more, so really think about what is really going on with your dog now. (Put yourself in their paws and see things from their point of view)
- Label and date the treatment bottle. It will keep for 30 days in the fridge. I recommend giving your dog 4 drops of these 4 times a day, it can be given on their food and on treats. Add 4 drops from the dosage bottle into a saucer of water and place this next to your dog's drinking water. This will give them the choice to self-medicate. If you are unable to do the 4 doses throughout the day, I suggest adding 4 drops from the dosage bottle into your dog's drinking water. This is because each time they have a drink they will be getting a dose of the magical crystal essence
- Mother tinctures will keep for many years as long as they are stored in a brown bottle and ideally out of the sun light. They are a very cost-effective way of having crystals essences easily available for your dog at any time that you may want to use a crystal essence. It would be also a good idea to label the mother tincture bottle with the properties of the crystal so that you can effortlessly reference which crystal essence to use.

Copyright Hoof and Paw 2019

How to make crystal water/essence by the indirect method

As I have said before, there are crystals that **cannot** be placed in water due to them being either poisonous or the water would damage them. There is however a method that allows crystal water/essences to be made safely. Again, the crystal must be cleansed and charged to gain maximum effect.

- Wait for a warm bright sunny day (The sun will be brightest at lunchtime) bring good intentions and a good heart.
- Crystals must first be cleansed and charged.
- Fill a glass bowl with cool boiled water.
- Place your chosen crystal in a 'drinking glass'.
- Then place the 'drinking glass' with the crystal into the bowl filled with water. This ensures that the crystal does not contact the water.

- Leave in the sun for three or four hours.
- If you want more potent water, then use more crystals of similar size.
- It will be difficult to cover with muslin, so strain the water into a jug using coffee filter paper,
- The crystal water should then be cooled and then placed in the fridge. Labelled and dated, it will keep for around 48 hours
- Pour into a bowl (not the dog's water bowl) as it is important for your dog to self-medicate ... Having a choice is the 'Key' to crystal healing.

HOW TO MAKE CRYSTAL WATER

This to me is by far the simplest way to offer crystal healing to your dog. It is **very** important though that you are aware of which of your crystals can directly be added to water. This is known as the 'direct method' of making up crystal water. Some crystals are poisonous, and some can be damaged by being placed in water. Please use my crystal guide for reference, as I have stated the correct method to use at the end of each description. I have made the following method **easy;** basically, dogs are not bothered about grids, meditating, dowsing or speaking to your spirit guide.

How to make crystal water/essence by the direct method

- Wait for a bright sunny day (lunch time is good) have positive intentions
- First, cleanse and charge your crystal of choice.
- Place the crystal in a glass bowl/jar and pour water over it. This must be water that has been previously boiled and then cooled.
- Put a piece of muslin over the top and secure with a band.
- Leave in the sunlight for three or four hours.
- If you want to make the crystal water more potent then use more crystals of similar size.
- The crystal water should then be cooled and placed in the fridge, labelled and dated. It will last for around 48 hours.
- Pour into a bowl (not the dog's water bowl) it is important for your dog to self-medicate ... trust me, they really do know better than us.

Copyright Hoof and Paw 2019

WHAT WATER DO I USE AS A CARRIER FOR THE ESSENCES?

This may sound like a strange question and it is one that needs careful thought. The energy of the crystal needs to have a perfect place to store their magical vigour. Humans are made up of 60% water and the earth is covered in over 60% water. Therefore, it makes total sense that water would be the best vehicle to store the beautiful crystal energy in. We may take water for granted but it is water that offers us our life force, we would not be able to survive if we did not have fresh drinking water.

There have been studies by the brilliant Professor Emoto who proved that the power of words had a huge impact on the way the crystals formed in water as it began to freeze. Water that was lovingly spoken to formed beautiful crystal shapes. Water that was shouted at formed deformed crystal shapes. If you just think about it, every glass of water from a tap in the UK has passed through someone else! They may have been happy or sad, the point is that their energy has imprinted on the water and is stored in the tap water that we drink. I highly recommend that water that is boiled and cooled should be used as a carrier for your crystal essence.

Water that is good for crystal essences

- Mains water that has been purified through a filter and then boiled and cooled, the boiling helps the water lose any stored information.

- Glass bottle mineral water with a mineral content of less than 200mg/l

Not good for crystal essences

- Mineral rich spring or mains water with a mineral content of 1000mg/l or more

- Water contained in plastic bottles can be contaminated by the plastic leaking into the water, so not recommended.

- Unfiltered water which is pumped through the water system under pressure makes water less able to absorb information.

This is an important thing to do as it activates the 'life force energy of the essence. You only need to shake the bottle 5 or 6 times and you must to do it each time before you give the essence to your animal. A treatment bottle (where the drops have been taken from a stock bottle and placed in a 30ml treatment bottle) will last for 3 weeks in the fridge.

- Why do some practitioners have different preferences and still get the same clinical result with various crystal essences?

All crystal essences have varying heightened healing qualities. The clinical application is influenced by the personal preference of the practitioner, but it does not mean that the result will be different. It is the combination and the intention of the choice of crystals that is the most important consideration.

- If a Crystal is obtained illegally is it still as effective?

This is correct in the sense that the individual's clearness of consciousness cannot function properly in such cases. This is even true if the individual is unaware that the crystal has been stolen, as crystals can amplify past energies. That is why it is so important that crystals are cleansed before use.

- How do you amplify Crystal essences?

The best way to amplify crystals and essences is to expose them to the rising sun for at least 2 hours. This is when the life force energy is at its most powerful. Meditate upon the crystal, connect to their energy, let your animal sit in the energy of the crystal.

- Is it a good idea to expose crystal essences to specific colours?

The wavelength of certain colours harmonizes with the crystalline structure of certain crystals such as clear quartz. Each colour has its own wavelength, animals see colours very differently to humans. Colour amplifies the crystals properties. The greater the harmony, the more the essence absorbs energy from the colour to release its healing qualities.

- How important is it to shake the crystal essence before giving it to your animal?

Facts about crystals that you may want to learn

- Does your positive or negative thoughts influence crystal healing?

As crystals are energy power houses, your thoughts can have an influence on the crystals. Always try to be balanced when doing crystal healing with an animal.

- Is there any difficulty in giving crystal essences to animals?

Not really but just remember not to put a pipette in their mouth as it may break. Don't leave loose crystals in hay or straw. Crystal essences work through certain parts of physical and subtle bodies and these can become blocked due to abuse, so the essences may take a little longer to work.

- What is the effect if the animal takes a large dose such as an entire bottle?

One drop or one gallon will work in the same way. The reason is that it is not the quantity that is important; it is the frequency with how it is taken. Crystals are called 'vibrational' medicines, which means that they work with the vibrations of your animal's aura, meridians and Chakra's.

- What is the recommended dose of a crystal essence?

Crystal essences should be taken at the stock/treatment level to work best. Further dilution would weaken the clinical properties. The recommended dose to give to animals is three to four times a day. The best time to give the essence is morning, lunch and evening. Give the essence for 3 or 4 weeks and then stop to see how your animal is getting on. Except where there are chronic conditions, animals can take the crystal essence for up to a year. I would suggest that if the condition has not improved considerably in that time, I would use a different crystal essence. Always seek veterinarian advice as your first port of call.

Copyright Hoof and Paw 2019

Program your crystal

What does it mean to program your crystal? You can program your crystal with 'your intentions' as crystals will amplify how you are feeling. This allows a massive scope for ideas. I personally believe that by treating my crystal with respect and love, they truly do understand this reverence. So, when I program my crystal with good intentions, my dreams do come true.

- The crystal needs to be cleansed and charged.

- You can program all crystals but the best crystal to use is a Clear Quartz. This is because it will hold your instructions for longer.

- Hold the crystal in your hand and just sit quietly with it for a few minutes. When you feel a connection to the crystal, say the following words.

"I ask with love and light and with the highest purpose, that this crystal is programmed with the intention of *state your intention*" Sit for a few more minutes with the crystal and then thank the crystal.

- You can ask your crystal to protect your dog from fleas
- Keep your dog safe when they are near roads
- To protect your dog from the neighbourhood bully
- Offer healing to your dog for specific problems

The uses are endless, anything you think of can be amplified through your crystal. You can place the crystal near where your dog sleeps or put it in a little pouch and attach it to their collar but please remember that dogs are very sensitive to energies. The crystal can be placed by the back/front door as your dog comes and goes. I personally like to place a crystal randomly in a room and let the dog choose their own healing.

- Charging your crystals in the moonlight is excellent for the crystals that fade in the sunlight. I like to wait for the full moon and mark this date on my calendar. This is so I have the perfect night offering my crystal the opportunity to bask in the beautiful moonlight.
- Now this method is for those of you who like excitement and a challenge. Place your crystal outside in a thunderstorm, when the energy is highly charged, and the rain is splashing everywhere. Be careful of the wind as it could displace your crystal. It is a well-known fact, that crystals like to return to the earth and will use any means to do it by. A stormy windy night would give them ample opportunities to make a run for it. I have had crystals that have literally disappeared. In my heart, I have always known that they have made it back to where they were birthed from.

There are a variety of ways to cleanse crystals, the most important thing to remember is that not all crystals like water and water can in fact damage them. Get to know your crystal by researching the best method cleansing for them. For the crystals listed in this workbook I have listed next to them the process you should use if you were going to make them into a crystal essence.

- Place your crystal in a bowl, sprinkle with sea salt, then pour water over the crystal and salt. Leave this in a cool place, away from animals and children. Then rinse under running water and allow it to dry naturally.
- For those crystals that don't like water, they will need to be 'smudged'. This is such a fun process and just involves lighting some incense sticks such as sage or sandalwood. Holding the crystal in the stream of smoke for a few minutes, having the intention of it being cleansed.
- Take your crystal for a day out to a beach and allow your crystal to soak in the sea water. Wash under fresh running water and allow it to dry naturally.
- Visualize your crystal being surrounded by a 'cleansing' bright white light and stay with this vision until you feel your crystal has been cleansed.

Charging your crystal

Once you have 'cleansed' your crystal you will then need to 'charge' your crystal. This basically means 're-energising' your crystal by re-connecting them to the energy of the 'earth', the 'sun' the 'moon'. This is a really simple process and it is up to you to decide on how you would like your crystal to be charged.

- Place your crystal outside in the sunlight, I like them to be outside for the day, but a couple of hours would be fine. It is important to remember that some crystals such as Amethyst, Citrine and Rose Quartz can lose their colour if left in the sunlight for too long. I have been asked many times about leaving the crystals on a window ledge to capture the sunlight. Personally, I like to take my crystals outside 'change of scenery' and all that. I do think that they appreciate extra efforts too. If, however you have no access to outside, then a window ledge will be fine.

Copyright Hoof and Paw 2019

Examples of some of the conditions that Crystal therapy may be good for:
- Aches, sprains and pains
- Muscular tension
- Injury
- Joint and skeletal problems
- Stress
- Anxiety
- Depression
- Trauma, both physical & emotional
- Aggression
- Hyperactivity
- Obsessive behaviour
- Training problems

The following indications are suggestions for using specific crystals for healing your dog. I have chosen crystals which are easy to obtain. As always, seek the best available competent medical advice for your dog. The information is not intended to replace the advice of a professionally qualified vet. Your vet always remains responsible for the health and welfare of your dog and should be first port of call if your dog is not feeling well.

CLEANSING–CHARGING-PROGRAM YOUR CRYSTAL

Cleansing

The way I see this process is to treat my crystals as if they were little 'people'. By nurturing and loving your crystal, they will work hard for you. Crystals will hold on to negative energy, therefore it is important to reflect on 'their' journey in life before they became part of your collection. Consider where it was mined and think about the big machine, ripping it from its home. It is then transported across the world. Every person that handles that crystal will imprint it with their energy. Think of how they may have been feeling that day; angry, sad, hateful, stressed, jealous or if it was a good day, they may have been happy. As your crystal sits in a shop, it will have been picked up by many people and experienced many things on its journey. You must therefore cleanse it of its 'negativity'. This is a very important step, as when you are using your crystals for animal healing it is a must that it will not be 'clogged' with negative energy.

CRYSTAL PROPERTIES

What are Crystals?

Crystals form naturally in the earth, whenever conditions allow. When molten minerals and superheated gases form the earth's mantle work their way outwards towards the surface through cracks, they start to cool. Molecules that make up these substances stop moving about randomly and start to group together into stable patterns. The molecules have set themselves into a completely even geometric shape. This is the basis of the crystal's structure. Depending on the conditions e.g. pressure, heat etc. the crystal may form a number of geometric shapes.

What is Crystal Energy?

Crystals have a charge and emit an energy vibration. Simplistically crystals emit a healing energy which resonates with human, animal or plant matter, to produce healing protective qualities.

What is Crystal Therapy?

Crystal therapy is an energy healing therapy that works with an animal's subtle energy fields to help address physical, emotional, mental and spiritual problems. Crystal therapy does not involve any pressure, manipulation or massage.

Crystal therapy has been used in many different cultures since ancient times. Crystals emit natural stable energy vibrations which affect an animal's energy fields and using specifically selected crystals helps to remove energy blockages within the chakras, meridians and subtle bodies to balance, heal and harmonize the body, mind and spirit.

The Benefits of Crystal Therapy

Stimulates and supports the body's natural ability to heal itself

- De-stresses, calms and detoxifies
- Provides relaxation and well-being
- Revitalizes, energizes and refreshes

Copyright Hoof and Paw 2019

CRYSTAL	PROPERTIES & USES
22. ZOISITE 	Zoisite is believed to be a natural detoxifier and can help to help reduce inflammation. It is said to stimulate fertility and can help heal diseases of the ovaries and testicles. In addition, Zoisite is thought to help recovery after trauma or severe illness. Zoisite is a slow acting crystal so therefore should be worn for long periods of time. *Indirect method*

Copyright Hoof and Paw 2019

CRYSTAL	PROPERTIES & USES
18. TIGER EYE	This crystal brings about calmness from chaos, it allows animals to enjoy being carefree. It is good for the treatment of eye disorders and broken bones and will help to strengthen the spinal column. This crystal dispels fear and anxiety. It is particularly useful for healing psychosomatic illnesses, dispelling fear and anxiety. *Indirect method*
19. SUGILITE 	Sugilite is today's "love stone", representing spiritual love. It opens the chakras up and brings them into alignment with the flow of love. It encourages positive thoughts, alleviating sorrow, grief and fear. Sugilite should be considered as the stone to use if your animal is in palliative care. *Indirect method*
20. TURQUOISE 	This powerful crystal is the crystal 'pet protector'. The turquoise crystal will protect your pet from the dangers and pollutants of city life. It will boost the confidence of your shy pet and stabilize mood swings. Turquoise can assist with creative problem solving and can calm the nerves. *Indirect method*
21. UNAKITE	This crystal helps animals deal with the past, it enhances weight gain, skin tissue and hair growth. Unakite supports convalescence & recovery from a major illness. It treats the reproductive system and stimulates healthy pregnancies while also facilitating the health of the unborn animal. If combined with Moonstone, it would offer powerful support during gestation. *Indirect method*

CRYSTAL	PROPERTIES & USES
15. ROSE QUARTZ 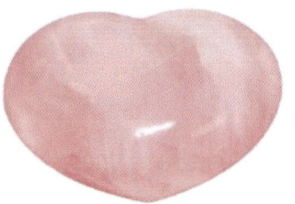	'This crystal is for the heart', it will help heal past abuse or cruelty. Rose Quartz helps animals to forgive and to let go of resentment. If your animal is aloof, lonely or isolated, Rose Quartz will help your animal learn the powers of love and gentleness, if you are inviting a new pet into a full household. This stone will help spread the love equally and facilitate harmony with all other animals. *Direct method*
16. SMOKEY QUARTZ 	This stone helps to heal disorders in paws, claws, and fins. It is very calming especially when your animal is stressed after an accident and will keep them remain calm until your vet arrives. Smokey Quartz helps heighten survival instincts. It is excellent for when your animal is experiencing changes to their life. It also helps with the nervous system and swellings. This wonderful grounding stone works slowly to eradicate negative energy and hostility. It would be a good crystal to use if your animal is aggressive to other animals. *Direct method*
17. SODALITE – BLUE 	This is a very calming crystal and is good for nervousness and will settle your animal down during travel, it is especially good for travel sickness. It is good for phobias and is especially useful should your animal should get panicky. It will boost their immune system and support the throat chakra. Sodalite will reduce the negative and enhance the positive side of life. It allows self-acceptance, self-esteem and self-belief in your animal's own abilities. Sodalite is often used for 'communication'. *Indirect method*

CRYSTAL	PROPERTIES & USES
11. JADE	Jade assists the immune system, kidney and heart. It is a good crystal to use at end of life situations. Jade aids the body's filtration and elimination organs. It is excellent for treating kidney problems and adrenal glands. Jade removes toxins, rebinds skeletal and cellular systems, and heals stitches. It assists fertility and childbirth. *Direct method*
12. LAPIS LAZULI	This stone is excellent for animals exposed to chemicals as it flushes toxins from the body. Lapis Lazuli is very protecting, revitalises and stimulates your pet. This stone strengthens the throat, bone marrow and immune system. Lapis is the strongest stone you can find to relieve the pain of leukaemia and bone cancer. It is good for low energy and depression. *Indirect method*
13. MALACHITE	Malachite has very high levels of copper and can lead to serious or *fatal blood poisoning* even if small amounts are swallowed. It helps animals who are in un-natural environments and those who suffer with arthritis and other painful conditions. It is good for obsessive behavior, epilepsy and aids liver detoxification. *Indirect method*
14. MOONSTONE	This crystal aids female problems such as hormone, mood swings, and stressful births. It will help mothers to connect to their offspring by helping them to bond. As the crystal name suggests, moon stone has an affinity with the moon cycles, as in period cycles. Use this crystal to bring calmness to any animals who are coming into season. *Indirect method*

Copyright Hoof and Paw 2019

CRYSTAL	PROPERTIES & USES
7. CITRINE	This stone strengths your animal's immune system and will help them to sleep. It helps with training problems. It supports animals that lack concentration. This energetic stone will aid their digestive track and alleviate their fears. It can be used to treat Alzheimer's as it helps to alleviate fears. *Direct method*
8. CLEAR QUARTZ	Master healer and the ultimate crystal to have in your collection. It is an excellent stone to use when 'programming' a crystal with your intentions, as it can hold onto your instruction for longer. It is effective for all conditions as it can amplify energy. When you place a quartz crystal around your pet's neck, it will increase his immunity, stimulate his thyroid and decrease respiratory problems. Clear Quartz amplifies communication between human and animals and strengthens mental clarity. *Direct method*
9. FLUORITE	As the name suggests, this crystal will help to strengthen bones and teeth. It comes in a range of colours; blue/green or clear. Clear aids respiration, green aids blood purification and is especially great for convalescing animals. Green/yellow aids the digestion of food. It carries a calm, stable frequency that brings order to chaos, and scattered and discordant energies into cohesion and harmony. *Direct method*
10. HEMATITE	As the name suggests is excellent for blood disorders. It can stem bleeding and is brilliant for keeping your animal grounded. It is excellent when there is a feeling of panic. Hematite stimulates iron absorption in the small intestine, which in turn improves the oxygen supply to the body. *Indirect method*

CRYSTAL	PROPERTIES & USES
4. BLACK TOURMALINE	This stone is an excellent protector of background radiation. It is grounding and protects animals from human stress, especially if they cannot get away from the source of anxiety. It offers relief to the animal if they suffer from aches and pains. Think of this as the protecting stone. *Indirect method*
5. BLOODSTONE	This crystal is as the name suggests good for blood disorders; anaemia, regeneration of cells, repair and renewal of wounds, mood stabiliser and any type of bleeding. Considerer using, if your animal has been poisoned, suffering from fatigue/exhaustion. This is an excellent stone for any animal recovering from an illness or operation. It is often used to purify and detoxify the body. Great at grounding negative energy and cleansing the body, Bloodstone brings love into any situation and helps ground the negative energies surrounding that issue. *Indirect method*
6. CARNELIAN	This crystal aids confidence, low self-esteem and releases sorrow as it helps to lift depression. It helps animals who have apathy and don't seem to be 'with it'. Think of this stone as your sunshine stone as it will bring a ray of sunshine to your elderly animal that may be fading in their final years. It helps animals who are lacking in focus and understanding. It is also good for animals that have a poor appetite and are feeling weak during an illness. This crystal is often called the 'sunny stone' due to its optimistic outlook on various situations that can happen in an animal's life. *Direct method*

CRYSTAL PROPERTIES & USES

When making a Crystal Water or Essence, some crystals are poisonous or delicate so need to be made up in a special way. (Indirect Method) The normal way is (Direct Method). The correct method is written in red after each Crystal description. Both methods will be described in detail further on in the manual.

CRYSTAL	PROPERTIES & USES
1. AMBER 	Amber improves throat difficulties such as asthma and respiratory problems. It can help kidney and bladder problems such as cystitis. This beautiful uplifting stone will revitalize the whole system. It also heals infections, allergies, digestive problems. It is the perfect stone to support your animal after an operation. *Direct method*
2. AMETHYST 	Amethyst helps animals to cope with bereavement and grief. It is a **must** stone for your collection. It is excellent for animals who suffer from separation anxiety as it helps them to deal with the stress. It is a very calming stone and will help your animal to relax. Amethyst is a powerful all-around healer. It is an excellent natural flea repellent as fleas hate the vibrations of amethyst. As it is a calming stone, it will help to calm down hot-headed animals, so aids any training. *Direct method*
3. AVENTURINE 	If your animal is fearful then this is the stone for you. It is excellent for rescue animals, as it works on past abuse. It helps to strengthen their blood, lungs, heart and adrenal glands. It will also strengthen your pet's nerve. It should always be considered for 'nervous' animals. Some varieties contain minerals that give it silver, brown, or occasionally red colours, although the green variety is the most common. *Direct method*

the memories of how they were birthed, which were sometimes very traumatic. Once loved and cherished they are happy to help in any way they can.

What is piezoelectricity?

Squeeze certain crystals such as clear quartz and it is possible to make electricity flow through them. Piezoelectricity is the appearance of an electrical voltage through the crystal when it is subjected to being squeezed (hardly, a human hand would 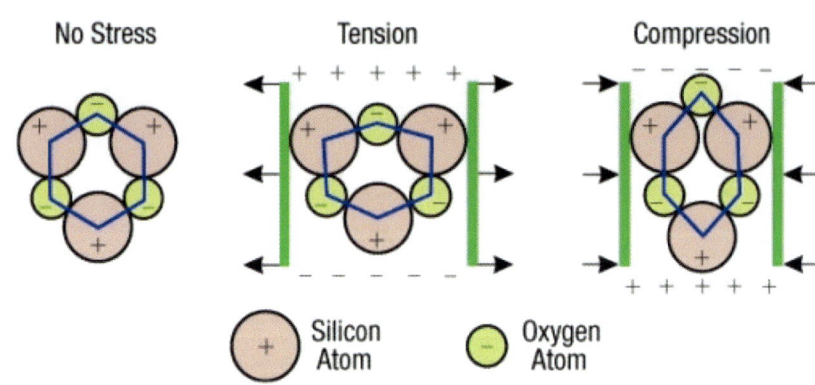 not be enough but when thrown onto another crystal, you would definitely see sparks). In essence your crystal becomes a tiny battery with a positive charge on one side and a negative charge at the other end

What causes piezoelectricity?

If we go back to my original description of the atom you will remember that the molecules are arranged in such a methodical way and this pattern is repeated endlessly. Although they are immovable, they can still vibrate. Normally, piezoelectric crystals are electrically neutral: the atoms inside them may not be symmetrically arranged, but their electrical charges are perfectly balanced: a positive charge in one place cancels out a negative charge nearby. However, if you squeeze or stretch a piezoelectric crystal, you deform the structure, pushing some of the atoms closer together or further apart, upsetting the balance of positive and negative, and causing net electrical charges to appear. This effect carries through the whole structure so net positive and negative charges appear on opposite, outer faces of the crystal. Piezoelectricity proves that crystal carry energy and can give out a specific frequency. In the quartz watch for example the piezoelectric effect is used to keep perfect time. Electrical energy from a battery is fed into the quartz crystal to make it oscillate exactly once per second, then 60 seconds per minute and so on. Clear Crystal quartz are brilliant crystals for amplifying the frequency of other crystals so are truly amazing when you are creating grids.

As well as the science behind crystals there is also the mutual respect for your crystals and the connection that you make with them. If you treat them with respect and understanding they will work hard for you. Remember they have been birthed from mother earth and they are the connection back to mother earth. They have stored

Copyright Hoof and Paw 2019

Choose a Crystal by labelling its properties helps you to learn!

Carnelian is an orange-coloured variety of Chalcedony, a mineral of the Quartz family.

The Carnelian crystal not only boosts courage and self-confidence, but on a cellular level it purifies the blood and improves circulation, a must-have for any stressful situation.

Sun Stone

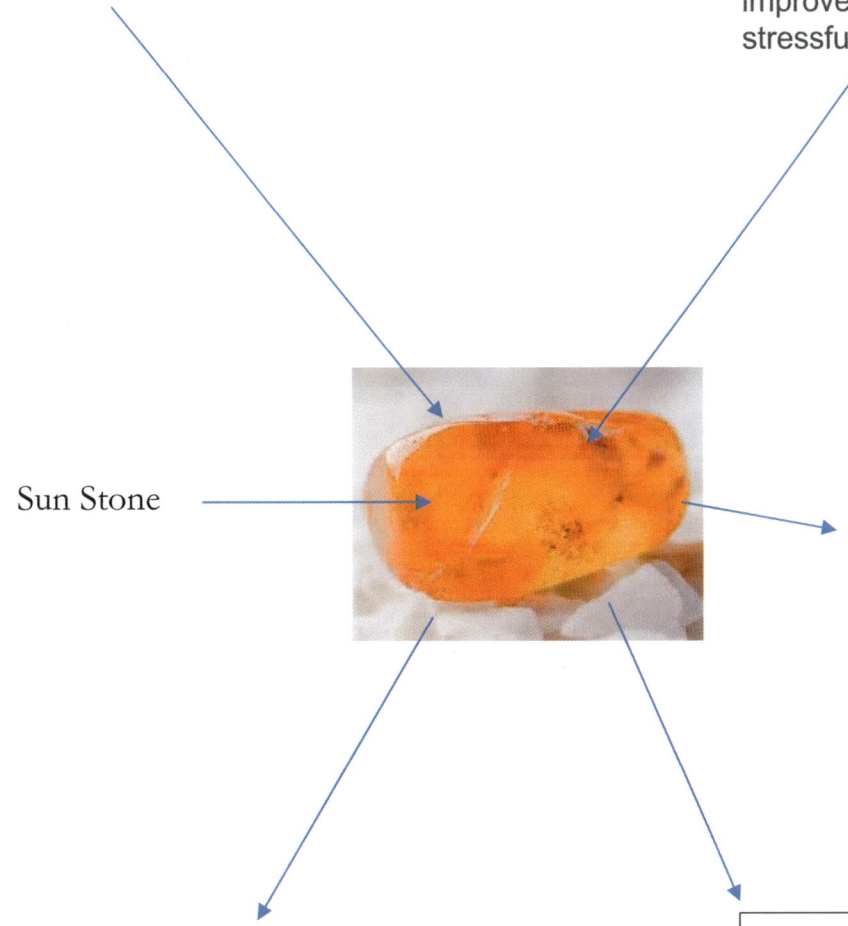

Known as a **stone** of motivation and endurance, leadership and courage, Carnelians have protected and inspired throughout history

The ancient Egyptians called Carnelian "the setting sun." In its orange hues, they identified it with the receptive or passive female energies, and associated it with the fertile menstrual blood of the mother goddess, Isis. In its red, red-orange to reddish brown shades, they considered it the active male energy stone, recognized by its glowing vibrant

Carnelian is composed of Silicon Dioxide and is a crypto crystalline quartz (Chalcedony) belonging to the Quartz group of minerals. This stone is formed when quartz crystals have iron impurities. The colour of the crystal depends on the level of iron in the crystal. Carnelian when place with other stones will clear them of negative energy.

Copyright Hoof and Paw 2019

chemical properties of differing crystals can definitely offer physical healing to the animal.

As we pass through a millennia of ages and believe that we are living in the most modern intellectual era, we have to be humbled by the fact that actually our science is now only just proving what we already knew. The scientific world is often mirroring the metaphysical world as it is demonstrating that the animal body has an electromagnetic force field when actually we already knew that our animals have an 'aura'. Science is really new, whereas metaphysical beliefs are very old and filled with knowledge. The ancients knew that 'crystals' held powers, they knew how to use them, and they knew that these powers could actually heal an animal.

Definition of a Crystal

Crystals have specific properties and make up that makes them so unique. They were birthed by mother earth and have spent many of millions of years being pushed and poked via the heating and cooling of the earth. A stone is a combination of different minerals but does not have a crystalline structure, such as lapis lazuli and hematite. All crystals are minerals but not all minerals are crystals. Crystals will keep growing in the same geometric formula by continually repeating its crystalline grid pattern. In is large form it is still the same crystal formation as in its minuscule form. Using the following SNIFC you will be able to know the difference between a crystal and other stones.

<u>S</u> Solid at room temperature and naturally occurring so it cannot be manmade

<u>I</u> Inorganic so it cannot come from something that is manmade such as cubic zirconia.

<u>N</u> Not organic so it cannot be made from resin or wood, such as amber or petrified wood.

<u>F</u> Formula of chemistry that never varies, if the crystal was cut in half one half would be a mirror image of the other half.

<u>C</u> Crystalline grid pattern that never varies, black obsidian would not qualify as that is a volcanic glass and moldovite does not theoretically qualify as it is not a mineral and does not come from this earth

However, it does not mean that stones such as lapis lazuli or the resin amber do not have their place in animal crystal healing. As I have said before, everything is energy, everything vibrates at a specific frequency. Just because it does not follow the SNIFC logic above it does not mean that the stone does not carry its own magical property.

Copyright Hoof and Paw 2019

which cannot be seen by the naked eye. It has been proven that all living organisms are made up of more than just cells they also have biophotons which are part of their DNA cellular system. They are like crystals as they are light emitting particles within your animal's body. You can actually get them to light up when quartz is brought into their aura. When your animal is well there are lots of them but when unwell the numbers are low. The beauty of crystal healing is that these biophotons get excited and energised by crystals. This is so exciting as it is more proof that crystals truly do interact with your animal's aura.

Everything is made of energy and crystals will help your animal to vibrate at different frequency's. To understand the structure of a crystal it is important to understand this on a microscopic level. This is a very basic description, but an atom is the smallest part of any matter. They have what looks like their own solar system. They have negative electrical particles called the electron which surrounds a nucleus containing positive electrical particles called protons. These negative and positive particles are always in balance as they are held together by neutral particles called neutrons to make sure that there is always balance. Atoms make up molecules and these make up the crystal structure that grows in 'constant' crystalline repetitive form. The atoms and molecules pack themselves SO closely together during their growth as they are held together by strong electromagnetic forces. The magic though is that in this compact space the electrons are in constant and rapid motion around the nucleus and this is where the 'energy' is being generated and repeated as it grows. In animals the hearts electromagnetic field is the strongest and being the biggest it can be easily influenced by emotional problems. This is where crystals such as 'rose quartz' will oscillate with the out of balance frequency of the animal to raise the vibrational frequency back to its normal range.

In the situation of crystals helping the physical body, this is where crystal therapy is fascinating. Crystals are made of mineral elements for example calcium which can actually help your animal physically. When you bring the energy of the crystal into your animal's aura it will act as an oscillator or more precisely a frequency stabiliser. The crystal will get your animals magnetic field/aura to resonate at exactly the same frequency. The calcium in the crystal will resonate with the calcium in your animal's system so it will perceive

that it has more calcium. Your animals' brain will respond to that by releasing chemicals in the brain to tell the animal that it is not calcium deficient. Basically, the

Copyright Hoof and Paw 2019

The Science Behind Crystal Healing

Our animals are often easily influenced by the comings and goings of the day, stress being a major contributor. Their electromagnetic field will resonate on a lower frequency if they feel, grief, sadness or if they are sick. Their normal frequency will then be knocked out of balance. In fact, anything can interact with their energy fields and leave its mark. As crystals are so geometrical perfect, they have the lowest possibility of being knocked off their frequency. And this is why it is so important to keep your crystals cleansed and charged as eventually too they will not be resonating at their base frequency. If your crystal is doing a lot of healing work, it too will get knocked out of its normal frequency. For crystals to work to their full potential you will need them to be at their best and caring for them correctly will make a huge difference. A crystal will vibrate at their own vibrational frequency dependent on their molecular makeup, their size, their thickness and their colour which would be their light frequency. Crystals on their own are not going to do all of the work as we need to add our intention to the healing as where thoughts go energy flows.

Clear Quartz has a grid structure so perfect and so precise that it never gets knocked from its normal frequency. Clear crystal quartz is a very powerful crystal. It is so easy to programme and can amplify the energy of other crystals. It is made up of the chemical formula silicone dioxide which is also known as silica. Scientists have discovered that human bodies are made up of liquid crystals that are sustained by silica. Your animal's cells too have their own magnetic field just like their body does, this is known as their aura. On a bigger scale the earth has its own magnetic field. Life cannot exist without silica. Silica is therefore an essential nutrient and plays a big part in your animal's cellular functions and is responsible for helping your animals' body to absorb other minerals. There have been experiments where cells

have been separated by a clear quartz and also by glass. The cells which were separated by the glass were not able to communicate but the cells separated by clear quartz were able to share vital information. A human body is made up of 7g of silica.

Light is also produced by your animal's cells and forms a way for your animal to connect to their environment. Your animal emits a low intensity glow

Copyright Hoof and Paw 2019

- Is your horse allowed to live with their pair bond/live in an established herd? A horse left on his own would be extremely stressed, as horses are prey animals. In the wild they would always be in a herd. More eyes to see the dangers!

- Does your dog get enough exercise? A pet that does not get enough exercise can become bored and frustrated. This could lead to them acting out behaviours which you may find undesirable.

- Your pet needs mental stimulation. This can be provided with a range of stimulating toys that you can use to play with them.

5. FREEDOM FROM FEAR AND DISTRESS

- What can cause your animal fear and distress? Puppies and kittens taken away from their mothers too young can become fearful and distressed as they have not had time to learn from their mother and siblings the skills to be a confident young animal in their own right.

- To prevent an adult pet from being unsure of himself and fearful, it is essential that he has been socialised to as many new experiences as possible during the critical socialisation period.

- Protect your pet by avoiding stressful situations.

With ownership comes great responsibility to meet the needs of your pet. In my view we owe it to them to truly recognize how our animal has evolved and how they are expected to cope in the modern world we live in. Love, excellent vet care, understanding them from an evolutionary point and outstanding nutrition are key to maintaining a healthy well-balanced dog.

2. FREEDOM FROM DISCOMFORT DUE TO THE ENVIRONMENT

- Does your animal have an appropriate shelter and environment which provides protection from temperature and weather extremes? Consider it from an animal's point of view. If whilst at work you have left the heating on and your animal gets too hot, does he have freedom to move somewhere cooler?

- Does your animal have a comfortable resting place of their own where they can feel safe and secure? It is especially important for older dogs/cats and puppies/kittens to have a quiet, safe area in an environment free from things that could cause harm.

3. FREEDOM FROM PAIN, INJURY OR DISEASE

- If your animal is unwell, it is important that they receive a rapid diagnosis by a qualified veterinarian. In the wild animals would seek out healing herbs to help heal any ailments. Animals living in our homes are 100% reliant on us to seek out the care they need.

- Does your animal see a veterinarian on an annual basis? Prevention is the key to keeping your animal well.

4. FREEDOM TO EXPRESS NORMAL BEHAVIOURS FOR THE SPECIES

- In the wild, horses would live in herds, dogs would live in packs.
  Does your animal have adequate opportunity to meet and interact with others of their own species? Dogs and cats are both social animals. Although we think we can speak dog or cat and think we know what they are saying and need, dogs and cats truly benefit from meeting animals of their own kind.

Copyright Hoof and Paw 2019

Brambell's Five Freedoms

For nearly all animals that have human caretakers, virtually everything in their lives is at their owner's mercy and out of the animal's control. What happens then is that the owner's predominant emotions and responses become the guidance mechanism for the animal as to when they need to experience any of the 5 Freedoms below. Also, what happens when the owner is unable to meet the freedoms? Animal cruelty? We have a huge duty to meet each freedom on a daily basis, so our animals are emotionally and physically healthy.

In 1965, Professor Roger Brambell was asked to investigate how animals are farmed intensively. This was the most comprehensive effort to define the basic needs of animals. As a result of his investigation Brambell made recommendations on how farm animals should be kept. "The 5 Freedoms", although initially for farm animals, can apply to all animals including cats, dogs and horses. They can help us assess how well we are meeting our animals' needs and therefore their welfare.

1. FREEDOM FROM THIRST, HUNGER AND MALNUTRITION

- Does your animal have access to fresh water?

- Does your animal have a wholesome diet that is natural to their species? Remember, it is us who chooses the time our animal eats and what they eat. So, looking at it from your animal's point of view, have we taken their free choice away?

- Do not over-feed your animal. In the wild animals would only choose to eat what they need and what is good for them. You would never find an overweight animal in the wild!

Copyright Hoof and Paw 2019

DOG BEHAVIOUR

Dogs are social species so need companionship from other dogs. In single dog only home, they transfer their need for companionship to people or other animals in the household, and this is perfectly normal behaviour. We becme part of their family as much as they become part of ours.

- They cannot be left alone for long periods of time as they crave companionship. If left on their own for long periods, it can lead to 'separation anxiety' which may lead to them barking, howling, digging or chewing.
- Dogs are hot-wired from wolves, so communicate in a very similar way, using visual signals such as submission, smelling each other, urine marking and vocalization.
- Dogs are pack animals, and recent research has shown that feral dogs form groups with a flexible hierarchy. It is importnant for humans to be consistent with the way they interact with their dogs, and to recognise dominant or guarding behaviour can become an issue, so they should ask for help if this happens.
- Dogs are territorial animals and will defend that territory if they feel threatened.
- Dogs need to be socialized from a young age, to other dogs, people and experiences. Or they may be fearful which could lead to fearful aggression.
  Dogs need to be exercised on a regular basis; they need to let off steam, to experience different smells and have the chance to meet other dogs. Sniffing is an important part of their exercise, so try to vary where you go so that they have new smells to sniff.
- It is important to recognise that different breeds are bred for different purposes. So may need altered types of exercise and stimulation to meet their individual needs.
- Dogs like a varied diet and can eat both meat and plants. If left to their own devices, they would scavenge almost anything; it is a natural trait which means they have been known to eat out of bins, if given the chance.
- Dogs like structure, consistency and fair discipline, and like to play too. In fact, they love to play.
- Dogs peak at dusk and dawn, so at these times they may be more excitable, barking, jumping or chewing.

Copyright Hoof and Paw 2019

INTRODUCTION

I have been working with crystals for many years, teaching lots of students how to use crystals with dogs. The most important thing for me is to make crystal healing fun and easy for you to understand; as I appreciate that it can be very overwhelming with knowing where to start. It is important to teach from experience and to share what I have learnt from the animals, always to remember that they know best. Left to their own devices in the wild, dogs have for thousands of years been able to medicate with herbs, choosing them for their individual healing properties. Connect to crystal energy by lying next to a rock or stone, with the properties they needed for curing. With the dew on the petals of certain flowers, dogs knew instinctively the flower essence properties contained and would eat the petals. I have often seen my dogs gently nibbling the flower heads, eating herbs from my garden and of course lying next to the crystals in my home, even carrying them in their mouth (which is not what I recommend but it shows that it is them choosing what crystal they would like to sit with today)

Today in our fast moving world, puppies are taken away from their mothers at a really young age before they learn how to be a dog. Play and correction from mum and socialization are so important, otherwise dogs are fearful. You have seen it so often where the fearful dog becomes aggressive as he does not like dogs invading his space. It is likely that he is unable to communicate with other dogs, as he has not learnt the skills, the language of dog. Yes! Dogs do have a language, a way to greet one another, to say hello, to say keep away. It was hot-wired from wolves and little has changed little over the millennium of years. With a little bit of understanding you too can read the language of dog.

We tell our dogs, where to sleep, what to eat, what time to eat, what time to walk, who to be friends with. We monitor where they can go, we have in essence manufactured a very un-natural world for them, polluting their environment with oven spray, furniture spray, bleach and chemical odours, to make our houses look clean and smell nice. Not so good for Fido I think but he has NO say in our choice of cleaning products.

CRYSTAL HEALING FOR DOGS
BY CAROLINE C THOMAS

CONTENTS

- Introduction
- Dog Behaviour
- Brambell's 5 Freedoms
- Crystal Science & Properties
- Choosing a Crystal for your Dog
- Cleansing and Charging Crystals
- How to make a Crystal Essence
- How to make a Crystal Grid
- How to use a Pendulum
- Balancing Your Dog's Chakra's
- My Yummy Crystal Recipe Combinations
- Twinkly Crystal Exercises
- Transition
- Crystal First Aid For Your Dog
- The Science of Crystal Grids

Caroline is a regular contributor to the 'Healthful Dog' Magazine, where eminent vets from around the world also share their holistic articles. Sharing the science of subjects such as Crystal Healing, Flower Essence Therapy and EFT to a wider audience, is what is at the root of Caroline's work. She was also a speaker at the World Holistic Pet Conference. Writing is one of her great passions and she has contributed many articles to spread the word about holistic therapies and animals.

Always make sure that you contact your vet as the first line of treatment if you have concerns about the health and welfare of your dog. Your vet always remains responsible for the health and care of your dog. Holistic therapies should always be used as complementary and not seen as an alternative.

This Book is a requirement of the Crystal Healing 4 Animals Course

www.emotionalhealing4animals.co.uk

Copyright Hoof and Paw 2019

were launched with Caroline's book at the 2017 Animal Energy World Conference. To gather the needed evidence Caroline has trialed the combination essences with over 100 domesticated dogs from around the world. Caroline published a scientific paper on October 2017, in the Healthful Dog Magazine. It contained all the evidence from trial, and it proved that flower essences really do work. 2017 was also the '50th' year of the creation of the Bailey essences. The Scintilla range is available from the Yorkshire Essence Website.

Caroline has written 2 fully accredited and insurable online Practitioner courses for Animal Bach Flowers and Crystal Healing Therapy. The courses also include a 1-2-1 with Caroline. She has an online academy, which allows her students to study with her via a private Facebook Page. Her dream is to raise the awareness of flower essences and crystals within the veterinary world, so that they are treated with respect and hold credibility. In her spare time Caroline makes candles and holistic animal healing pendants and collars for dogs and cats also rhythm beads for horses. Caroline has been happily married for over 25 years and has two sons, two Spaniels and three cats.

ABOUT CAROLINE

Caroline has been working with flower essences and animals for over 15 years. She initially qualified as a Bach Flower Practitioner and then as an Animal Bach Flower Practitioner via the Bach Flower Centre in Oxford and then at the Natural Animal Centre in Wales. Caroline is an Animal Reiki teacher and was taught by Kathleen Prasad, whose teachings push the understanding of Reiki with animals to the highest levels. Caroline went on to study PsychAromatica with Nayana Morag which uses aromatherapy to get to the root of any problem an animal may have. Using Traditional Chinese Medicine Techniques. Nayana specializes in Meridians and this is where Caroline developed her interest in EFT and is now a member of the Guild of Energists.

Caroline continued to work with Bach flowers and became very passionate about helping animals with mental health issues. Partly driven by her own experiences which affected her earlier in her life, she has been helping animals with extreme emotional and behavioral problems using flower essences with much success. Caroline is a Registered Pharmacy Technician and manager at a busy Doctors surgery in Essex. She applies the same approach to her staff and patients and has filled her office with crystals and flowers, where many a time GP's who are passing, have popped into her office and have said that they can feel the calm loving energy.

Caroline has followed closely the works of Arthur Bailey, who was the founder and creator of the Bailey essences. She was fascinated by his down to earth approach and his scientific mind. He created many of the essences on the Ilkely moors and Caroline loved his passion for flower essences and the clever way that he created them. Caroline contacted the Bailey Essences and was given permission to write a book about how they can help animals. The book is called the Power of Bailey, Bach and Verbeia Essences for Animals and it is available via Amazon. It is a beautiful book filled to the brim with everything that you need to know about flower essences and how to use them with animals.

The Yorkshire Essences asked Caroline to develop a range of '7' combination essences for specific animal behaviours which were called the Scintilla range, they

NOTES

Index

A

abdomen, *57, 59*
ABUSE, *91*
Achilles, *57*
acupuncture, *69*
agate, *56*
Amazonite, *58*
AMBER, *17, 95*
AMETHYST, *17, 95*
AVENTURINE, *17, 95*
Azurite, *53*

B

Bloodstone, *18, 59*

C

Coral, *53*

E

Emerald, *47*
endocrine, *59*

F

FLUORITE, *19, 95*

H

HEMATITE, *19, 95*

J

Jadeite, *72*

L

LAZULI, *20, 95*

M

MOONSTONE, *20*

O

Obsidian, *54, 59, 77*

P

pancreas, *46, 57*

Q

QUARTZ, *19, 21, 95*

R

rescue, *17, 43, 81*
rheumatism, *76*
Rhodochrosite, *54, 81*

S

SMOKEY, *21*
SODALITE, *21, 95*
spinal, *22, 46*
SPLEEN, *57*
STOMACH, *56*
SUGILITE, *22, 95*

T

topaz, *64*
TURQUOISE, *22, 95*

Z

zirconia, *13*
ZOISITE, *23, 95*

Printed in Great Britain
by Amazon